The Least
You Should Know
about Vocabulary Building
WORD ROOTS

The Least You Should Know about Vocabulary Building WORD ROOTS

Sixth Edition

Teresa Ferster Glazier
Late, Western Illinois University

Carol E. Friend
Mercer County Community College

Laura D. Knight
Mercer County Community College

WADSWORTH
CENGAGE Learning

Australia • Brazil • Japan • Korea • Mexico • Singapore • Spain • United Kingdom • United States

WADSWORTH
CENGAGE Learning

The Least You Should Know about
Vocabulary Building: Word Roots,
Sixth Edition
Teresa Ferster Glazier, Late, Carol E. Friend,
and Laura D. Knight

Publisher: Lyn Uhl

Acquisitions Editor: Annie Todd

Editorial Assistant: Dan DeBonis

Senior Technology Project Manager:
    Stephanie Gregoire

Marketing Manager: Kate Edwards

Marketing Assistant: Kate Remsberg

Advertising Project Manager:
    Darlene Amidon-Brent

Content Project Manager: Sarah Sherman

Senior Art Director: Cate Rickard Barr

Print Buyer: Betsy Donaghey

Rights Acquisition Account Manager:
    Lista Person

Production Service/Compositor:
    ICC Macmillan Inc.

For product information and technology assistance,
contact us at
Cengage Learning Customer & Sales Support,
1-800-354-9706
For permission to use material from this text or product,
submit all requests online at **cengage.com/permissions**
Further permissions questions can be emailed to
permissionrequest@cengage.com

Library of Congress Control Number: 2007921902

ISBN-13: 978-1-4130-2958-1

ISBN-10: 1-4130-2958-2

Wadsworth
25 Thomson Place
Boston, MA 02210
USA

Cengage Learning is a leading provider of customized learning solutions with office locations around the globe, including Singapore, the United Kingdom, Australia, Mexico, Brazil, and Japan. Locate your local office at: **international.cengage.com/region**

Cengage Learning products are represented in Canada by Nelson Education, Ltd.

For your course and learning solutions, visit **academic.cengage.com**

Visit our corporate website at **cengage.com**

Printed in Canada
3 4 5 6 7 09 08

Contents

To the Instructor

When we were approached to create the revision for *The Least You Should Know about Vocabulary Building: Word Roots*, we thought about how we could improve upon a tried-and-true text. After careful study, we decided to add two new roots, to update the exercises, including adding word root review exercises earlier in the text to reinforce learning, and to incorporate the word roots into students' long-term memory. We maintained the original format because it is successful as it stands.

Because learning to break words into their parts is perhaps the most important initial step in vocabulary building, this text helps students take that step and begin what should become an ongoing study of words. Whether the text is used in the classroom or for self-help, the following features make it easy to use with little guidance.

1. Because only one approach is used—word roots—students can work through the text easily. They learn a method of study while learning the first root and follow it throughout the book.

2. No distinction is made between Greek and Latin roots. Students need to remember the meaning of a root rather than its language source. Similarly, no distinction is made among roots, prefixes, and suffixes because all are equally sources of word meaning.

3. Students learn words in context. After a word is defined, it is then used in a sentence.

4. Some difficult words are included for those who happen to be ready for them, but students should be encouraged to concentrate on words they have encountered before and are curious about.

5. The simplest pronunciation aids are used; the only diacritical mark being the one for long vowels.

6. A Word Index simplifies using the text.

A packet of ready-to-photocopy tests is available to instructors on adoption of the text and may be obtained from the local representative or from the English Editor, Wadsworth, 25 Thomson Place, Boston, MA 02210.

Acknowledgments

Thanks to our colleagues at Mercer County Community College and our families for their support, and to Teresa Glazier for creating *The Least You Should Know . . .* series.

—Carol E. Friend and Laura D. Knight

Increasing Your Vocabulary through Learning Word Roots

How did words get to be words? Why, for example, is a hippopotamus called a hippopotamus and not a glipserticka? There's a good reason. Since the animal looks a bit like a fat horse and spends much of its time in rivers, the Greeks combined their word for horse, HIPPOS, and their word for river, POTAMOS, and called the animal a hippopotamos, a river horse. And with only a one-letter change, the word has come down to us as hippopotamus.

Words did not just happen. They grew. And if you learn how they grew—what original roots they came from—you'll find it easier to remember them. You'll *understand* the words you look up in the dictionary instead of just memorizing the definitions. And weeks later, even though you may have forgotten the meaning of a word, your knowledge of its roots[1] will help you recall its meaning.

The best first step in vocabulary building, then, is to become familiar with some word roots because learning the root of one word often gives a clue to dozens or hundreds more. For example, if you learn that SYN (SYM, SYL) means *together* or *with*, you have a clue to more than 450 words, for that many words beginning with SYN (SYM, SYL) are listed in *Webster's Third New International Dictionary*. Similarly, when you learn that *philanthropist* is made up of PHIL *to love* and ANTHROP *human*, you have learned not only that a philanthropist is a lover of humanity, but you also have a clue to some 70 other words beginning with PHIL and to more than 60 others beginning with ANTHROP, not to mention those that have PHIL or ANTHROP in the middle or at the end of the word.

As you become aware of how words are made up, familiar words will take on new meaning, and unfamiliar words may often be understood even without a dictionary. For instance, if you know that the root BIBL means *book* as in *bibliography* and *Bible*, then you can guess that a *bibliophile* will have something to do with books. And if you remember that PHIL means *to love*, as in *philanthropist* (lover of humanity), then you will immediately guess that a bibliophile must be a lover of books.

Glancing at the root chain following this paragraph will help you spot some common roots. The chain begins with *biped* [BI two + PED foot], a two-footed animal. The next word contains one of the preceding roots, PED. A *pedometer* [PED foot + METER measure] is, as its roots indicate, "a foot measure" or an instrument that measures the distance walked by recording the number of steps taken. The next word must contain METER, and out of the hundreds of METER words, *geometry* [GEO earth + METER measure] has been chosen. As its roots show, geometry was originally a system of "Earth measuring," that is, of measuring the Earth through the use of angles. The next word must contain GEO, and so on.

---

[1] In this book, the term *roots* includes prefixes and suffixes because all word parts are equally sources of word meaning. All are the roots from which our language came.

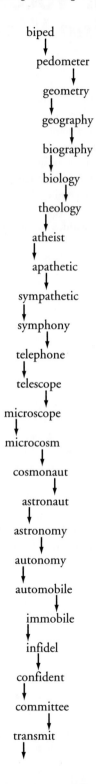

transport
↓
report
↓
recur
↓
excursion
↓
exclude
↓
seclude
↓
secure
↓
manicure
↓
manuscript
↓
subscribe
↓
subversive
↓
controversy
↓
contradict
↓
benediction
↓
benefactor
↓
facilitate

This root chain ends with *facilitate* (to make easier). Perhaps reading the chain will facilitate your spotting word roots in the future.

After you've learned some of the roots in this book, try to make a root chain of your own.

Learning word roots is not only the quickest way to increase your vocabulary but also the most entertaining. For example, did you know . . .

that **salary** [SAL salt] originally was the money paid to Roman soldiers to buy salt . . .
that a **companion** [COM with + PAN bread] was originally a person one shared one's bread with . . .
that **malaria** [MAL bad + AER air] was so named because people thought it was caused by the bad air of the swamps . . .
that a **terrier** [TERR earth] got its name because it digs in the earth after small animals in burrows . . .

that **escape** [ES out + CAP cape] originally meant to get out of one's cape, leaving it in the hands of the pursuer . . .

that an **insect** [IN in + SECT to cut] was so named because its body is "cut" into three segments . . .

that a **bonfire** in the Middle Ages was the bone fire built to dispose of corpses during the plague . . .

that **panic** originally described the frantic efforts of the Greek nymphs to escape when the mischievous god Pan suddenly appeared among them . . .

that **curfew** in the Middle Ages in France was the ringing of a bell telling the peasants to cover their fires (*couvre-feu*) for the night . . .

that **alphabet** comes from the first two letters of the Greek alphabet, ALPHA and BETA, "a" and "b" . . .

that **trivia** [TRI three + VIA way] in Roman times meant the crossroads where three ways met and where neighborhood gossips on their way to market often stopped to chat about unimportant things (TRI VIA talk) . . .

that **preposterous** [PRE before + POST after] originally meant having the before part where the after part should be, like a horse with its tail where its head should be—in other words, absurd.

As you look up words in your dictionary, you may uncover other interesting stories if you note the word roots, which will be found in square brackets either just before or just after the definition.

Where to Find Word Roots in Your Dictionary

Most dictionaries give the derivation (word roots) of words. You'll find the derivation either just after or just before the definition.

The American Heritage Dictionary, 4th College Edition[1]

> **eu·pho·ny** (yōō′fə-nē) *n., pl.* **-nies**. Agreeable sound, esp. in the phonetic quality of words. [Fr. *euphonie* < LLat. *eupho-nia* < Gk. < *euphōnos*, sweet-voiced : *eu-*, good + *phōnē*, sound.]

The derivation is in square brackets at the end of the definition. The last part of the derivation gives the original roots: *eu-*, good + *phone*, sound.

Webster's New World Dictionary, 3rd Edition[2]

> **eu·pho·ny** (-nē) *n., pl.* **-nies** [Fr. *euphonie* < LL. *euphonia* < Gr. *euphōnia* < *euphōnos*, sweet-voiced, musical < *eu-*, well + *phōnē*, voice: see PHONE¹] the quality of having a pleasing sound; pleasant combination of agreeable sounds in spoken words; also, such a combination of words

The derivation is in square brackets before the definition. The last part of the derivation gives the original roots: *eu-*, well + *phone*, voice.

Webster's 11th New Collegiate Dictionary[3]

> **eu·pho·ny** \′yü-fə-nē\ *n, pl* **-nies** [F *euphonie*, fr. LL *euphonia*, fr. Gk *euphōnia*, fr. *euphōnos* sweet-voiced, musical, fr. *eu-* + *phōnē* voice — more at BAN] (ca. 1623) **1 :** pleasing or sweet sound; *esp* : the acoustic effect produced by words so formed or combined as to please the ear **2 :** a harmonious succession of words having a pleasing sound —

The derivation is in square brackets before the definition. The last part of the derivation gives the original roots and the meaning of one of them: *phone*, voice. To find the meaning of the other root, look for *eu-* as a regular dictionary entry. There its meaning is given: well or good.

Thus, the roots indicate that *euphony* means good sound or good voice. And when you look at the definitions, you'll find that that is exactly what it means: agreeable sound; the quality of having a pleasing sound; pleasing or sweet sound. Having learned the roots of *euphony*, you'll remember the word longer than if you had merely looked up the definition.

Changes in Root Spelling

A root may change its spelling slightly according to the word it is in. For example, EX *out* is found in **excursion**, but it changes to ES in **escape** and to simply E in **educate**. Such changes have occurred to make pronunciation easier. Escape and educate are easier to pronounce than excape and exducate would be. Here are some of the ways root spellings change.

Sometimes the last letter of a root changes to be like the first letter of the root that follows:

COM nect	becomes	CON nect
COM loquial	becomes	COL loquial
COM relate	becomes	COR relate
DIS fident	becomes	DIF fident
SYN metrical	becomes	SYM metrical

Sometimes the last letter of a root changes (or is dropped) to make the pronunciation easier, but it doesn't become the same as the first letter of the root that follows:

EX cape	becomes	ES cape
COM temporary	becomes	CON temporary
SYN pathy	becomes	SYM pathy
DIS vert	becomes	DI vert
EX ducate	becomes	E ducate

A root may also appear in slightly different forms in different words. CLUD, *to close, to shut,* may appear as

CLUD	in	seclude
CLUS	in	recluse
CLAUS	in	claustrophobia
CLOS	in	closet

but you'll soon learn to spot a root even when its spelling varies.

How to Use This Book

It makes little difference which root you study first because each root will eventually help you with some new word. Therefore, the roots in this text are presented alphabetically.

As you work through the book, you may come across words with which you are unfamiliar. This is to be expected and will make studying this book challenging and rewarding. Working with word roots and the words that are formed from the roots will make your learning easier. After you learn the roots, you will notice that you can figure out the meaning of other words. Mastering even a few words under each root will boost your vocabulary.

Here are six steps to take as you begin your study:

1. First, take the PRELIMINARY TEST on page 8. At the end of your study, you'll have a chance to take similar tests to see how the study of word roots has increased your vocabulary.

2. Now turn to the first root—A, AN on page 12.

   (For help with pronunciation see the **Pronunciation Key** on the inside front cover of this book.)

   Note that not every root of every word is explained but only those that will help you remember the word.

   The first definition is often a literal one (marked *lit.*) taken directly from the meaning of the roots. The definitions that follow are current ones.

3. After you have studied all the words on the page, do Exercise 1 and correct your answers by checking the Answer section beginning on page 155.

4. Study again any words you missed—if they are ones you want to add to your vocabulary.

5. Next use some of the words in your own writing. Begin to keep a vocabulary journal, writing two or three sentences each day about whatever interests you and using some of the words you have just learned. Putting the words into your own writing will help you remember them longer than if you merely fill in blanks. From time to time, you can reread your journal to review your words.

6. Finally, take the most important step in vocabulary building—use your newly learned words in conversation. Using a word in conversation will do more to help you remember it than any amount of silent study. *Use a word three times and it's yours.* Try using one new word a day. Begin at breakfast, and during the day find two more opportunities to use the word. After you have used it three times, you'll be surprised how easily it will slip into your conversation. Even if it's a word you don't expect to use, it will stay in your passive vocabulary so that you'll recognize it when you encounter it in your reading.

PRELIMINARY TEST

Test yourself on these words taken from college textbooks and current magazines. Check your answers with those on page 155.

1. _____ **ambiguous** **A.** very large **B.** having two possible meanings **C.** seeking fame **D.** exceptionally clear

2. _____ **philanthropic** **A.** unmoved by criticism **B.** fond of animals **C.** sociable **D.** charitable

3. _____ **antipathy** **A.** strong dislike **B.** worry **C.** kindly feelings **D.** ancient times

4. _____ **autonomous** **A.** self-governing **B.** governed by a few **C.** governed by a dictator **D.** without any government

5. _____ **benefactor** **A.** one who receives money from a will **B.** one who receives a grant **C.** distant relative **D.** one who gives assistance

6. _____ **anachronism** **A.** mistake in grammar **B.** something out of its proper historical time **C.** incorrect calculation **D.** clock for navigation

7. _____ **circumscribe** **A.** to overcome circumstances **B.** to write an autograph **C.** to restrict the action of **D.** to denounce

8. _____ **convivial** **A.** sociable **B.** superficial **C.** dangerous to life **D.** vivid

9. _____ **credulous** **A.** unbelieving **B.** believing too readily **C.** suspicious **D.** having a good credit rating

10. _____ **precursor** **A.** supervisor **B.** beginner **C.** forerunner **D.** financial officer

11. _____ **pandemic** **A.** causing illness **B.** causing a wild uproar **C.** undemocratic **D.** widespread

12. _____ **euphemism** **A.** substitution of a pleasant for an unpleasant word **B.** substitution of a specific term for a general one **C.** false statement **D.** unrestrained praise

13. _____ **enervate** **A.** to weaken **B.** to strengthen **C.** to soothe **D.** to excite

14. _____ **epilogue** **A.** speech at a funeral **B.** speech at the end of a play **C.** speech at the beginning of a play **D.** speech of apology

15. _____ **loquacious** **A.** full of life **B.** having the ability to see through things **C.** understanding several languages **D.** talkative

16. _____ **malinger** **A.** move slowly **B.** spend too much time on details **C.** pretend to be ill to get out of work **D.** waste time

17. _____ **missive** **A.** lost article **B.** missing part **C.** wrong answer **D.** letter

18. _____ **metamorphosis** **A.** life of a butterfly **B.** change of form **C.** mental illness **D.** abnormal growth

19. _____ **panacea** **A.** remedy for all ills **B.** folk remedy **C.** widespread epidemic **D.** view from a mountain

20. _____ **apathy** **A.** dislike **B.** strong interest **C.** indifference **D.** sympathy

21. _____ **impediment** **A.** lack of funds **B.** hindrance **C.** inability to speak **D.** inability to walk

22. _____ **progeny** **A.** plan of action **B.** gifted child **C.** descendants **D.** ancestors

23. _____ **assiduous** **A.** overbearing **B.** haughty **C.** critical **D.** persevering

24. _____ **auspicious** **A.** unfavorable **B.** favorable **C.** foreboding evil **D.** having doubts

25. _____ **subterranean** **A.** under cover **B.** under the ocean **C.** under the earth **D.** underhanded

26. _____ **supercilious** **A.** haughty **B.** socially prominent **C.** intellectually superior **D.** solicitous

27. _____ **syndrome** **A.** place where horse races are held **B.** stadium **C.** two adjoining domes **D.** symptoms occurring together

28. _____ **telepathy** **A.** communication through means other than the senses **B.** walking in one's sleep **C.** an optical instrument used to view the stars and planets **D.** radio waves

29. _____ **tortuous** **A.** a large turtle **B.** full of twists and turns **C.** severe mental or physical pain **D.** large and foreboding

30. _____ **vocation** **A.** time off **B.** pastime **C.** territory **D.** profession

31. _____ **avert** **A.** to pay attention to **B.** to turn toward **C.** to turn away from **D.** an advertisement

32. _____ **veracious** **A.** honest **B.** inaccurate **C.** unhappy **D.** fanciful

33. _____ **tripartite** **A.** twisted **B.** two-prong spear **C.** composed of three parts **D.** a three-legged camera support

WORD ROOTS IN ALPHABETICAL ORDER

A, AN—not, without; unusual or irregular

When A or AN meaning *not* or *without* comes at the beginning of certain words, it gives those words a negative meaning. Anything that is **asymmetrical** is *not* symmetrical, and anything that is **atypical** is *not* typical.

Atheist and **agnostic** both begin with the negative A and are close in meaning. An atheist [A without + THE god] is *without* a God, whereas an agnostic [A not + GNOS to know] does *not* know whether there is a God. In other words, the atheist is sure there is no God, whereas the agnostic simply does not know.

Note how A or AN gives each of the following words a negative meaning.

agnostic (ag nos´ tik) [A not + GNOS to know]—one who does not know whether there is a God. *He had lost his former faith and had become an agnostic.*

amoral (ā mawr´ ul)—*lit.* without moral standards; neither moral nor immoral; unable to distinguish between right and wrong. *Infants are amoral.*

anarchy (an´ ur ke) [AN without + ARCH ruler]—*lit.* without a ruler; political disorder and confusion. *The overthrow of the government resulted in anarchy.*

anecdote (an´ ik dot) [AN not + EKDOTOS given out]—originally, not published (some stories were made public by publishing them, and others were kept private); now, merely a short account of some interesting or humorous incident. *The speaker enlivened his talk with humorous anecdotes.*

anemia (un ne´ me uh) [AN without + HEM blood]—*lit.* without blood; a deficiency of red corpuscles in the blood. *Her weakness was caused by anemia.*

anesthetic (an is thet´ ik) [AN without + ESTHET feeling]—*lit.* without feeling; a drug causing one to be insensitive to pain. *Before the operation, he was given an anesthetic.*

anomaly (uh nom´ un le) [AN not + HOMO same]—*lit.* not the same (as others); a rare exception; something that is not normal. *Charles Darwin wrote, "There is no greater anomaly in nature than a bird that cannot fly."*

anonymous (un non´ uh mus) [AN without + ONYM name]—*lit.* without a name; having an unknown or unacknowledged name. *The donor of the new building wished to remain anonymous.*

asymmetrical (ā si met´ ri kul) or asymmetric [A not + SYM together + METER measure]—*lit.* not measured together; not having both sides exactly alike; not symmetrical. *She preferred asymmetrical flower arrangements.*

atheist (ā the ist) [A without + THE god]—*lit.* one who is without a God; one who denies the existence of God. *As an atheist, she objected to the nativity scene in the town square at Christmas.*

atypical (ā tip´ i kul)—not typical. *A classical concert performed by a rock group would certainly be atypical.*

ALSO: amorphous, analgesic, apathetic, apathy, atom. (Look in the Word Index on page 177 for these words. Some are discussed under their other roots.)

✏️ **EXERCISE 1**   Write the appropriate A, AN word. Answers to the exercises are at the back of the book.

1. To add interest, the professor sprinkled her lectures with _____.
2. Jolene cried when she saw her _____ haircut: one side was three inches longer than the other.
3. The bidder at the auction wished to remain _____.
4. Bryn was late to class, which was _____ of her behavior.
5. _____ reigned when the protesters ran wild through the streets shouting slogans, breaking windows, and overturning cars.
6. After 10 years, Jose quit the ministry and announced he was now an _____ because he no longer believed there was a God.
7. Sheila is an _____, not knowing whether there is a God.
8. The mass murderer was _____, so he was judged unaccountable for his actions.
9. The dentist gave the patient _____ before pulling all her teeth.
10. To fight her _____, the doctor prescribed iron pills.
11. The socialite is usually so gracious that her leaving without even saying thank you was an _____.

✏️ **EXERCISE 2**   Match each word with its definition.

1. _____ agnostic   **A.** unusual or irregular
2. _____ atypical   **B.** one who denies the existence of God
3. _____ anarchy   **C.** an amusing story
4. _____ atheist   **D.** one who does not know whether there is a God
5. _____ anecdote   **E.** political disorder

✏️ **EXERCISE 3 JOURNAL**   The best way to remember new words is to use them immediately in your writing and speaking. Therefore, it's a good idea to keep a *vocabulary journal* in which you write two or three sentences daily using some of your new words. If you write about things that interest you, then you'll be inclined to reread your journal occasionally as a review.

AMBI, AMPHI—around, both

In Roman times, candidates for public office, wearing white togas so that they could be easily seen, walked *around* (AMBI) talking to people and seeking votes. Before long, the term *ambitio* took on the meaning of bribery in seeking votes, but by the time the word came into English in the fourteenth century as **ambitious**, it had lost the idea of seeking votes or of bribery and meant merely "eager to succeed or to advance."

ambience (am´ be uns) [AMBI around]—the surrounding atmosphere. *The long pictures on the walls and the paper lanterns gave the restaurant an oriental ambience.*

ambiguous (am big´ yO us) [AMBI around + AGERE to drive]—*lit.* to drive around (in an uncertain manner because there were few roads in early days); uncertain; having two possible meanings. *From her ambiguous answer, I couldn't tell whether she was complimenting or insulting me.*

ambitious (am bish´ us)—originally, going around for votes; today, having a desire to succeed. *She's ambitious and hopes to get a better job.*

amphitheater (am fuh the´ uh tur)—an oval or round structure with tiers of seats around an open space. *The Drama Department presented* Antigone *in the university amphitheater.*

In the preceding words, AMBI or AMPHI means *around.* In the following words, it means *both.*

ambidextrous (am bi dek´ strus) [AMBI both + DEXTR right hand]—*lit.* both right hands; able to use both hands with equal ease. *Because she is ambidextrous, she plays a great game of tennis.*

ambiguity (am bi gyO´ uh te) [AMBI both]—the quality of having two possible meanings. *The ambiguity in his writing leaves the reader puzzled.*

ambivalence (am biv´ uh luns)—conflicting (both kinds of) feelings toward a person or thing. *The boy was experiencing ambivalence about giving his speech, wanting to give it and yet dreading it.*

ambivalent (am biv´ uh lunt)—having conflicting (both kinds of) feelings toward someone or something. *A child often feels ambivalent about a new baby in the family, both liking it and resenting it.*

amphibian (am fib´ e un) [AMPHI both + BIO life]—an animal that lives both in the water and on land. *Frogs, toads, and salamanders are amphibians.* Also, an aircraft that can take off and land both on water and on land.

amphibious (am fib´ e us) [AMPHI both + BIO life]—able to live or to travel both on land and in water. *The Marines went ashore in amphibious vehicles.*

✏️ **EXERCISE 1**   **Match each word with its definition. There is one extra word.**

A. ambience   **C.** ambivalent   **E.** amphibian   **G.** ambidextrous
B. ambitious   **D.** amphitheater   **F.** ambiguous

1. _____ having conflicting feelings toward a person or thing
2. _____ having two possible meanings
3. _____ able to use both hands with equal ease
4. _____ an open structure with tiers of seats around an open space
5. _____ having a desire to be successful
6. _____ an animal that lives on both land and water

✏️ **EXERCISE 2**   **Write the appropriate AMBI, AMPHI word.**

1. The _____ of the country lodge was warm and friendly.
2. The hovercraft is an _____ vehicle.
3. Ben didn't stop writing when he broke his right arm because he is _____.
4. Jenna's _____ about hosting the Garden Club's party was obvious; she was both excited and nervous.
5. Herpetologists study frogs and other _____.
6. The town built an _____ so the theater members would have a place to perform their plays.
7. The witness's statement was filled with _____, so the police did not know whom to arrest.
8. Josh frequently stays late studying at the library; he is very _____.
9. His _____ answer left me wondering which door to open.
10. Being afraid of heights but loving adventure, she was _____ about learning to fly a plane.

✏️ **EXERCISE 3 JOURNAL**   **Write three sentences in your *vocabulary journal* using some of the AMBI, AMPHI words you have learned. Check with the sentence given in the explanation of each word to make sure you are using the word correctly. For example, *ambiguous* is an adjective, whereas *ambiguity* is a noun. But even without thinking about the parts of speech, you'll use the words correctly if you follow the model sentences.**

ANN, ENN—year

Words containing ANN or ENN will have something to do with *year*. An **anniversary** is the return of some event every *year*. An **annuity** is a fund that pays a person money every *year*. **Annual** means happening every *year*, and **semiannual** means happening every half *year*. **Biannual** and **biennial** are easily confused because they both come from BI *two* and ANN or ENN *year*. Just remember that **biannual** and **semiannual** (both meaning twice a year) sound alike, whereas **biennial** (meaning every two years) sounds different.

annals (an´ uls) [ANN year]—a written account of events year by year; historical records. *We searched the annals of the medical society to find when the vaccine had first been tested.*

anniversary (an uh vurs´ uh re) [ANN year + VERS to turn]—the yearly return of the date of some memorable event. *We're making plans for our parents' wedding anniversary.*

annual (an´ yO ul) [ANN year]—yearly. *We have an annual family reunion.* Also, lasting only one year, as an annual plant. *She liked annual plants even though she had to replace them every year.*

annuity (uh nO´ uh te)—an investment that provides fixed payments yearly or at other regular intervals. *After paying into his annuity for years, he now receives a check every month.*

biannual (bi an´ yOul) [BI two + ANN year]—occurring two times a year. *The treasurer made biannual reports in January and July.*

biennial (bi en´ ē ul) [BI two + ENN year]—occurring every two years. *The society holds a biennial convention in the odd-numbered years.*

centennial (sen ten´ ē ul) [CENT hundred + ENN year]—a hundredth anniversary. *The Exposition in Montreal in 1967 celebrated the centennial of Canadian Confederation.*

millennium (muh len´ ē um) [MILLI thousand + ENN year]—a period of a thousand years; specifically, the thousand years when, according to the New Testament, Christ is to reign on Earth; thus a period of happiness and prosperity. *Some reformers today are hoping for nothing short of a millennium.*

per annum (pur an´ um) [PER through + ANN year]—by the year; annually. *The chairperson received a fixed salary per annum.*

perennial (puh ren´ ē ul) [PER through + ENN year]—having a life cycle lasting through more than two years, as a perennial plant. *In his garden, he planted only perennials so that he wouldn't have to replant every year.* Also, lasting many years, as perennial youth. *She was a perennial student, still taking courses after she was 50.*

semiannual (sem ē an´ yO ul) [SEMI half + ANN year]—half yearly; occurring two times a year. *He made semiannual reports in January and July.*

superannuated (sO pur an´ yO ā tid) [SUPER above + ANN year]—*lit.* beyond the year of retirement; retired because of age. *Now that he was superannuated, he had time for his hobbies.*

ALSO: anno Domini (abbrev. A.D.), bicentennial, triennial

EXERCISE 1   Which ANN or ENN word names or describes the following?

1. yearly _____
2. occurring two times a year _____
3. hundredth anniversary _____
4. retired because of age _____
5. period of a thousand years _____
6. by the year _____
7. a written account of events year by year _____
8. having a life cycle lasting more than two years _____
9. the yearly return of a memorable event's date _____
10. an investment that provides fixed payments _____

EXERCISE 2   Write the appropriate ANN/ENN word.

1. Rita cleans her house _____, spring and fall.
2. The _____ celebration is held on every even-numbered year.
3. Anoke's _____ pays him $500 a month.
4. The _____ *of Joseon Dynasty* are records of Korean history.
5. The _____ teacher bored her friends with her long lectures.

EXERCISE 3 REVIEW   Fill in the blanks with words from the last three sections.

1. That two-headed chicken is certainly an _____.
2. The _____ candidate attempted to shake the hands of everyone who attended the rally.
3. David was _____ about taking the job overseas.
4. Luckily, our plane was _____ because we had to land on the lake.
5. Mark Twain's most humorous _____ were published in a book last year.
6. Phong is taking iron pills to alleviate his _____.
7. New City had a parade to celebrate its _____ anniversary.
8. Salamanders and other _____ fascinate my younger brother.
9. Juanita and Jose celebrated their fiftieth wedding _____ with family and friends.
10. Rebekah's garden is filled with _____ flowers because she likes her plants to return each year.

ANTE, ANTI—before

The ANTE spelling always means *before*—either *before* in place or *before* in time. **Anteroom** and **anterior** are *before* in place, whereas **ante** and **antedate** are *before* in time.

ante (an´ te) [ANTE before]—the amount each poker player must put into the pot before receiving his cards. *Feeling confident, he upped the ante.*

antecedent (an tuh sēd´ unt) [ANTE before + CED to go]—anything that logically goes before something else. *Cricket was the antecedent of baseball.* Also, the word, phrase, or clause to which a pronoun refers. *In the sentence "Every boy was in his place,"* boy *is the antecedent of the pronoun* his.

antedate (an´ ti dat)—to occur before something else. *The Revolutionary War antedates the Civil War.*

ante meridiem (an ti muh rid´ ē um) (abbreviated A.M.) [ANTE before + MERIDI noon]—before noon. *I have an appointment at 10 A.M.*

anterior (an tir´ ē ur)—located before or in front (as opposed to posterior, located behind). *The anterior legs of the kangaroo are shorter than the posterior ones.*

anteroom (an´ ti rOm)—a room before the main room; a waiting room. *In the director's anteroom were a dozen actors waiting to try out for the part.*

A variant spelling—ANTI—also means *before* in time in the following words.

anticipate (an tis´ uh pāt) [ANTI before + CAP to take]—*lit.* to take before; to realize beforehand. *No one anticipated such an outcome.*

antiquarian (an ti kwer´ ē un)—one who collects or studies objects of former times. *The antiquarian appraised the rare first edition of Sandburg.*

antiquated (an´ tuh kwa tid)—so old as to be no longer useful. *The factory had to replace the antiquated machinery.*

antique (an tek´)—belonging to an earlier (before) period. *In the parade were a dozen antique automobiles.*

antiquity (an tik´ wuh tē)—ancient (before) times. *The museum specializes in armor from antiquity.*

(ANTI meaning *against* or *opposite* will be found on page 22.)

✏️ **EXERCISE 1**   Write the appropriate ANTE, ANTI word.

1. Using _____ methods, the novelist handwrites her books with pencil and paper.
2. The doctor's _____ was filled with waiting patients.
3. The _____ oak desk sold for $1,000 at the auction.
4. None of us _____ a traffic jam at 4 A.M.
5. While Bill shuffled the cards, each player placed his _____ on the table.
6. Only the _____ of the house was damaged in the fire.
7. The _____ bookseller displayed his copy of *Huckleberry Finn* in the store window.
8. Ariel didn't _____ the party in her honor.
9. The history professor studied the pottery shards from _____.
10. I wake up at 7 _____ to walk the dog.

✏️ **EXERCISE 2**   Write C if the ANTE, ANTI word is used correctly.

1. _____ The taxidermist learned that the head is the anterior and the rump is the posterior.
2. _____ As an early riser, I make my appointments for the ante meridiem.
3. _____ In her Modern History class, she studied antiquity, especially the Gulf and Iraqi Wars.
4. _____ The jury was held in the antecedent before entering the courtroom.
5. _____ The children didn't anticipate the long line at the movie theater.

✏️ **EXERCISE 3 JOURNAL**   Write three sentences in your *vocabulary journal* using some of the ANTE, ANTI words you have learned. Check with the sentences given in the explanation of each word to make sure you are using the word correctly.

ANTHROP—human

Knowing that ANTHROP means *human* clarifies the meaning of a number of words. **Anthropology** [ANTHROP human + -LOGY study of] is a study of the development and behavior of *human* beings. A **philanthropist** [PHIL to love + ANTHROP human] loves *human* beings and promotes *human* welfare by charitable acts or gifts. A **misanthrope** [MIS to hate + ANTHROP human], on the other hand, hates *human* beings.

anthropoid (an´ thruh poid) [ANTHROP human + OID resembling]—resembling humans. *Gorillas, chimpanzees, orangutans, and gibbons are anthropoid apes.*

anthropologist (an thruh pol´ uh jist) [ANTHROP human + -LOGY study of]—one who studies the physical, social, and cultural development and behavior of human beings. *The anthropologist Margaret Mead lived for a time in Samoa studying the Samoan culture.*

anthropology (an thruh pol´ uh je) [ANTHROP human + -LOGY study of]—a study of the physical, social, and cultural development and behavior of human beings. *The anthropology professor commented that Eskimos have many words for snow.*

anthropomorphic (an thruh po mawr´ fik) [ANTHROP human + MORPH form]—thought of as having human form or characteristics. *The animal characters in Beatrix Potter's* Peter Rabbit *are anthropomorphic, speaking and acting like humans.*

anthropomorphism (an thruh po mawr´ fiz um) [ANTHROP human + MORPH form]—the attributing of human form or characteristics to a god, animal, or inanimate thing. *Anthropomorphism is a part of many primitive cultures, with rivers, trees, and animals being given human characteristics.*

misanthrope (mis´ un thrōp) [MIS to hate + ANTHROP human]—one who hates people. *Only a misanthrope would have such a low opinion of the human race.*

misanthropic (mis un throp´ ik) [MIS to hate + ANTHROP human]—characterized by hatred or scorn for people. *Ebenezer Scrooge shows his misanthropic attitude when he replies to a Christmas greeting with "Bah! Humbug!"*

philanthropic (fil un throp´ ik) [PHIL to love + ANTHROP human]—charitable. *The United Fund aids many philanthropic organizations.*

philanthropist (fi lan´ thruh pist) [PHIL to love + ANTHROP human]—one who loves people, particularly one who gives money to benefit humanity. *Andrew Carnegie, a famous philanthropist, gave money to build public libraries.*

philanthropy (fil lan´ thruh pē) [PHIL to love + ANTHROP human]—the effort to increase the well-being of humanity by charitable donations. *The corporation was known for its philanthropy as well as for its good business practices.*

✏️ EXERCISE 1   Write the appropriate ANTHROP word.

1. The animal characters in folktales are _____.
2. Bill Gates, a(n) _____, gives millions of dollars to charity each year through his foundation.
3. The _____ devoted his life to studying the Mayan civilization.
4. His neighbors branded him a(n) _____ because of his hateful attitude.
5. The gorilla's _____ features reminded Joe of his Uncle Fred.
6. The local soup kitchen is one _____ organization that fills a need in the community.
7. Many hope to change the world for the better by their _____.
8. Many folktales use _____.
9. The _____ woman lived alone in a rural area.
10. The _____ professor's essay "Body Ritual Among the Nacerima" is a humorous look at the culture of the United States.

✏️ EXERCISE 2 JOURNAL   In your *vocabulary journal,* write four sentences using ANTHROP words. Pick words that you have trouble remembering.

✏️ EXERCISE 3 REVIEW   Give the meaning of each root and a word in which that root is found.

ROOT	MEANING	WORD
1. A, AN	_____	_____
2. AMBI, AMPHI	_____	_____
3. ANN, ENN	_____	_____
4. ANTE, ANTI	_____	_____
5. ANTHROP	_____	_____

ANTI—against, opposite

ANTI meaning *against* is easy to spot in such words as **antifreeze, antitrust,** and **antisocial,** but it can also help clarify more difficult words.

A couple of ANTI words, which you probably won't have occasion to use and which won't be included in any of the tests in this book, are interesting just because of their stories.

Antipodes (an tip′ uh dez) [ANTI opposite + POD foot] means literally "with the feet opposite" and refers to any place on the *opposite* side of the Earth since the people there seem to be standing upside down with their feet *opposite* to ours. The British refer to Australia and New Zealand as the Antipodes because those countries are on the *opposite* side of the Earth.

Another word with an unusual history is **antimacassar** (an ti muh kas′ ur). In the nineteenth century, men used macassar oil, imported from Macassar, Indonesia, as a hair dressing, and the oil often left grease spots on the back of upholstered chairs where the men rested their heads. Their wives, therefore, made small covers to put on the backs of the chairs to keep the macassar oil from soiling the upholstery. The covers were called antimacassars [ANTI against + MACASSAR macassar oil]. Gradually all covers protecting the backs and arms of upholstered furniture came to be called antimacassars.

antagonist (an tag′ uh nist) [ANTI against + AGON struggle]—a person one struggles against in a contest. *The young wrestler was stronger than his antagonist.*

antagonize (an tag′ uh nīz) [ANTI against + AGON struggle] the act of incurring or provoking hostility. *Pulling its tail will antagonize the cat.*

antibiotic (an ti bi ot′ ik) [ANTI against + BIO life]—a substance produced by a microorganism that destroys other harmful (living) microorganisms. *Penicillin is an antibiotic.*

antidote (an′ ti dōt) [ANTI against + DOT to give]—a medicine that counteracts (works against) poison or disease. *After the snake bit him, he was quickly given an antidote.* Also, something that gives protection against injurious effects. *Plentiful jobs are one of the best antidotes to crime.* Also, something that gives relief against something else. *The comedy was a pleasant antidote to all the tragedies we had seen.*

antipathy (an tip′ uh thē) [ANTI against + PATHOS feelings]—a strong feeling of dislike. *Although a soldier, Mel felt no antipathy toward his opponents.*

antiseptic (an tuh sep′ tik) [ANTI against + SEPT putrid]—against infection; capable of destroying microorganisms that cause disease. *The nurse washed the wound with an antiseptic solution.*

In the preceding words, ANTI means *against*; in the following words it means *opposite*.

Antarctica (ant ark′ ti kuh)—[The vowel (i) is dropped when second syllable begins with a vowel (a)] the continent opposite the Arctic. *The Arctic is the region at the North Pole; Antarctica is the continent opposite it at the South Pole.*

anticlimax (an ti klī maks)—*lit.* the opposite of the climax; a sudden drop from the important to the commonplace. *Her present uninteresting job is an anticlimax to a brilliant career.*

uantithesis (an tith′ uh sis) [ANTI opposite + THES to place]—*lit.* one idea placed opposite another; the exact opposite. *Love is the antithesis of hate.* Also, ideas contrasted in balanced phrases, as *"To err is human; to forgive, divine."*

ALSO: antacid, antiphonal, antitoxin, antonym. (Look in the Word Index on page 177 for these words. Some are discussed under their other roots.)

EXERCISE 1   Match the ANTI word with its definition.

_____ 1. antagonize	**A.**	the continent opposite the Arctic
_____ 2. antipathy	**B.**	a medicine that counteracts poison
_____ 3. antibiotic	**C.**	a sudden drop from importance to commonplace
_____ 4. antiseptic	**D.**	a person one struggles against
_____ 5. anticlimax	**E.**	to provoke hostility
_____ 6. antagonist	**F.**	a substance produced by a microorganism that destroys other harmful organisms
_____ 7. antidote	**G.**	the exact opposite
_____ 8. Antarctica	**H.**	a strong feeling of dislike
_____ 9. antithesis	**I.**	against infection

EXERCISE 2   Write the appropriate ANTI word.

1. His dull closing speech was an _____ to the inspiring program.
2. The _____ lotion prevented the open wound from becoming infected.
3. The man who challenged him to a fight was a powerful _____ .
4. The continent of _____ surrounds the South Pole.
5. Diseases that were once fatal can now be cured with _____ .
6. Having an interesting hobby is an _____ to boredom.
7. A simple life is the _____ of a complicated one.

EXERCISE 3   On one of the blank pages at the end of this book, start a WORD LIST of words you hope to use in the future. Keeping a word list is an excellent way to increase your vocabulary; rereading your list occasionally will bring to mind words you might otherwise forget. Review the pages you've already completed for words with which you would like to start your WORD LIST.

AUTO—self

AUTO, meaning *self*, was a common Greek root, but it took on added meaning in America in the late nineteenth century when it was applied to the new vehicle that could "move by itself"—the automobile [AUTO self + MOB to move].

autocracy (aw tok′ ruh sē) [AUTO self + CRAT to rule]—government by a single person. *The country had become an autocracy and was ripe for revolt.*

autocrat (aw′ tuh krat) [AUTO self + CRAT to rule]—an absolute ruler; a domineering, self-willed person. *When the autocrat took over the country, the people lost all their power.*

autocratic (aw tuh krat′ ik) [AUTO self + CRAT to rule]—*lit.* ruling by oneself; domineering. *The supervisor was autocratic, accepting suggestions from no one.*

automatic (au tuh má tik) [AUTO self + MAT to act]—operating by itself. *The car has automatic transmission.*

automation (aw tuh ma′ shun) [AUTO self + MAT to act]—a system using self-operating machines. *The factory introduced automation and replaced many workers with robots.*

automaton (aw tom′ uh tun) [AUTO self + MAT to act]—an apparatus that functions by itself; a robot. Also, a person who has lost all human qualities and acts mechanically. *Because she had been stapling pages for so many hours, she felt like an automaton.*

automobile (aw′ tuh mō bēl) [AUTO self + MOB to move]—*lit.* a self-moving vehicle. *The Model T was one of the first automobiles.*

autonomic (aw tuh nom′ ik) [AUTO self + NOM law]—pertaining to the autonomic nervous system, which acts according to its own (self) laws rather than through voluntary control. It regulates the heart, digestive system, and so forth. *He was trying to learn to control the actions of his autonomic nervous system through biofeedback.*

autonomous (aw ton′ uh mus) [AUTO self + NOM law]—self-governing. *Released from state control, the college finally became autonomous.*

autonomy (aw ton′ uh me) [AUTO self + NOM law]—the right of self-government. *Many small nations are struggling for autonomy.*

autopsy (aw′ top sē) [AUTO self + OP sight]—*lit.* a seeing for oneself; an examination of a dead body to discover the cause of death. *The autopsy revealed that the cause of death was a heart attack.*

ALSO: autobiography, autograph, automat

✎ **EXERCISE 1**   Write the appropriate AUTO word.

1. The medical examiner performed an _____ on the murder victim to determine the exact cause of death.
2. The _____ lights go on when the electronic sensor is tripped.
3. The islanders overthrew the dictator to achieve _____.
4. The _____ nervous system controls the heart and digestive system.
5. He was _____ in his control of the firm, allowing others no power.
6. She was so tired that she appeared to be an _____.
7. After breaking away from the central governing body, the church became _____.

✎ **EXERCISE 2 REVIEW**   Write a C in front of each sentence in which all the words are used correctly.

1. _____ After days of traveling across Antarctica, the explorers finally reached the North Pole.
2. _____ The biannual meeting is held in June and December.
3. _____ The secretary summarized the year's events for the society's annals.
4. _____ For visual variety, the interior designer arranged the pictures in an asymmetrical pattern.
5. _____ Antiquity means "in the present."
6. _____ She knew her false rumors would antagonize her classmates.
7. _____ The Gulf War antedates World War I.
8. _____ Ambivalence means having two conflicting emotions at the same time.
9. _____ The elderly woman relied on her annuity to provide a fixed income every month.
10. _____ An agnostic does not believe in God.
11. _____ He presented a convincing argument against his antagonist's ideas.
12. _____ The antiquarian book buyer looked through my collection, but he didn't find any books new enough to interest him.
13. _____ The mother of the slain soldier felt antipathy toward the government that sent him to war.
14. _____ A misanthrope honored the cancer society with a generous donation.
15. _____ Falsehood is the antithesis of beauty.

✎ **EXERCISE 3 REVIEW**   As a review of some of the roots you have learned, try to make a root chain similar to the one on pages 1–3. Start with a word like *autobiography*, and refer to the preceding pages to find the words you need. You may have to make several starts before you get a chain of the length you want. When you are satisfied, copy your chain to one of the blank pages at the end of this book.

BENE—well, good

Words that begin with BENE always describe something *good*—an action, a result, or an attitude.

benediction (ben uh dik′ shun) [BENE good + DICT to speak]—*lit.* a speaking of good wishes; a blessing. *After the benediction, the congregation filed out.*

benefactor (ben uh fak′ tur) [BENE good + FAC to do]—*lit.* one who does something good; one who gives help or financial assistance. *The college owed much to its generous benefactors.*

beneficence (buh nef′ uh suns) [BENE good + FAC to do]—*lit.* the doing of good; kindness; charity. *The scholarships were funded through the beneficence of the alumni.*

beneficial (ben uh fish′ ul) [BENE well + FAC to do]—producing benefits; advantageous. *Having a study schedule is beneficial.*

beneficiary (ben uh fish′ e er e) [BENE good + FAC to do]—a person who receives benefits, as from a will or an insurance policy. *He was the beneficiary of his father's will.*

benefit (ben′ uh fit) [BENE well + FAC to do]—anything that promotes well-being; a payment to one in need. *She received considerable benefits from her exercise program.*

benevolence (buh nev′ uh luns) [BENE well + VOL to wish]—an inclination to do good; a kindly or charitable act. *The benevolence of the church members was shown by their generous contributions to charity.*
(Benevolence and beneficence are close synonyms.)

benevolent (buh nev′ uh lunt) [BENE well + VOL to wish]—*lit.* wishing someone well; inclined to do good. *The department manager had a benevolent attitude toward her staff, giving them days off now and then.*

benign (bi nīn′)—harmless; having a kindly (good) attitude or disposition. *The parents looked upon the capers of their son with benign tolerance.* Also, in medicine, mild in character; not malignant. *The growth proved to be benign rather than malignant.*
(Benevolent and benign are close synonyms. Both mean having a kindly attitude, but benevolent often includes the idea of doing something charitable, and benign often has a medical meaning opposite to malignant.)

ALSO: beneficent

✎ EXERCISE 1   Match the BENE word with its definition.

1. _____ benevolent   **A.** advantageous
2. _____ benediction   **B.** inclined to do good
3. _____ benign   **C.** one who does good
4. _____ beneficial   **D.** a blessing
5. _____ benefactor   **E.** harmless

✏️ **EXERCISE 2**   Write the appropriate BENE word.

1. Nutritionists really do recommend eating "an apple a day" because eating it is
_____.

2. As the only child, Kelly is the sole _____ of her parents' estate.

3. The congregation rose for the _____.

4. Alec's _____ nature is obvious from his charity work.

5. The employee's medical _____ paid for his surgery.

6. The alumni's _____ provided the money for the scholarships.

7. Gina's doctor reassured her that the tumor was _____.

8. The homeless family was given shelter and food through the _____ of the charity.

9. The anonymous _____ funded the town's library.

✏️ **EXERCISE 3 REVIEW**   Write a C in front of each sentence in which all the words are used correctly. Then, in the remaining blanks, write the word that should have been used.

1. _____ Ten college scholarships were funded through the philanthropy of the large corporation.

2. _____ Prosperity is an antagonist for political unrest.

3. _____ The anthropology class was studying the Native American Navajo culture.

4. _____ Instruments today can measure the functioning of the autonomous nervous system.

5. _____ The chimpanzees and other amphibians were playing in the trees.

6. _____ After being a British colony for years, the island finally achieved autonomy.

7. _____ Having no interest in his job, he worked like an automaton.

8. _____ Jeet received a stated salary per annum plus a benefits plan.

9. _____ When the trick-or-treaters knocked at his door, the benevolent neighbor shouted for them to go away.

10. _____ The ambitious student finished her BA degree in three years.

✏️ **EXERCISE 4 JOURNAL**   Add three words that you have found difficult to your *vocabulary journal;* then write sentences that show the meaning of each. Adding words to your journal on a regular basis will make a great difference in your word power.

BI—two

Back in the days of sailing ships, according to one story, the bread taken along on the voyages always became moldy. Then someone discovered that by baking the bread *twice*, enough moisture could be removed so that it remained edible during long voyages. The new kind of bread was called *biscuit* [BI two + COQUERE to cook] or *twice*-baked bread. Today, biscuits are no longer twice-baked but are merely quick breads or nonyeast breads baked in small cakes.

bicameral (bi kam´ ur ul) [BI two + CAMER chamber]—composed of two legislative chambers or branches. *The United States has a bicameral legislative system composed of the Senate and the House of Representatives.*

bicentennial (bi sen ten´ ē ul) [BI two + CENT hundred + ENN year]—a 200th anniversary. *The United States celebrated its bicentennial in 1976.*

bicuspid (bi kus´ pid) [BI two + CUSPID point]—a tooth having two points. *A human adult has eight bicuspids.*

bigamy (big´ uh me) [BI two + GAM marriage]—marrying one person while legally married to another. *Bigamy is against the law in this country.*

bilateral (bi lat´ ur ul) [BI two + LATER side]—having or involving two sides; binding on both parties (in contrast to unilateral, in which only one party has an obligation). *According to a bilateral agreement, each of the two nations will cut armament expenditures.*

bilingual (bi ling´ gwul) [BI two + LINGU language]—able to use two languages. *In Canada, job opportunities are greater for a bilingual person.*

bipartisan (bi pahr´ tuh zun)—consisting of or supported by two parties, especially two major political parties. *Assured of bipartisan support, the senator was confident the bill would pass.*

biped (bi´ ped) [BI two + PED foot]—a two-footed animal. *Humans are the only bipeds who laugh.*

biscuit (bis´ kut) [BI two + COQUERE to cook]—*lit.* twice-cooked or baked; today a quick bread baked in small pieces. *The biscuits were soft and chewy.*

bisect (bi´ sekt) [BI two + SECT to cut]—to cut in two, as a diameter bisects a circle. *The nature trail bisects the park.*

bivalve (bi´ valv)—a mollusk having two valves or shells hinged together, as a mussel or clam. *The oyster is a bivalve that is valued by both gourmets and jewelers.*

ALSO: biannual, biceps, bicycle, biennial, bifocal, binoculars, bigamist, binomial, bipartite

✎ **EXERCISE 1**   Write the appropriate BI word.

1. The dentist recommended a root canal for Curt's _____ because the root was infected.

2. Because her mother speaks Spanish and her father speaks English, Maya is _____.

3. Both houses in our _____ system must pass laws.

4. Sean, Mary's husband, committed _____ when he married Susan as well.

5. The _____ bill easily passed both houses of Congress.

6. A _____ celebration occurs every two hundred years.

7. Signed by both countries, the agreement was _____.

8. Men and monkeys are both _____.

9. The winding river _____ the state.

10. Bernie steamed and ate his favorite _____, the clam.

✎ **EXERCISE 2**   Underline the appropriate BI word.

1. The United Kingdom has a (bicameral, bilingual) system of government.

2. Suri's (bivalve, bicuspid) broke when she fell off her bicycle.

3. Some computer programs allow (biped, bilingual) students to answer in either of their languages.

4. The next (bipartisan, bicentennial) celebration for the club will be in 2008.

5. The United States outlawed (bigamy, bipartisan) in 1862.

✎ **EXERCISE 3 JOURNAL**   In your *vocabulary journal,* write five sentences that you might use if you were writing a paper about Congress. Use as many BI and BENE words as possible.

BIO—life

The root BIO, meaning *life*, combines with SYM, meaning *together*, to form an interesting word—**symbiosis**, the living together of two dissimilar organisms, usually for the benefit of both. For example, the hermit crab lives among the lethal tentacles of the sea anemone and is protected from its enemies by the stinging power of the tentacles. The anemone, on the other hand, is carried in the claws or on the back of the hermit crab to new feeding grounds. Thus the symbiosis is beneficial to both.

autobiography (awt uh bī ahg′ ru fē) [AUTO self + BIO life + GRAPH to write]—an account of a person's life written by that person. *The Autobiography of Benjamin Franklin is a classic.*

biodegradable (bi ō di gra′ duh bul)—capable of being broken down by living microorganisms and absorbed by the environment. *She switched to a biodegradable detergent, which would not pollute the streams.*

biofeedback (bi o fed′ bak)—a technique for consciously regulating a bodily (life) function thought to be involuntary, as heartbeat or blood pressure, by using an instrument to monitor the function and to signal changes in it. *She found that she could slow her pulse by using biofeedback.*

biography (bi ahg′ ru fē) [BIO life + GRAPH to write]—a written account of someone's life. *Carl Sandburg wrote in his biography of Lincoln: "When he kept store he often held an open book in his hand, reading five or ten minutes, closing the book to wait on a customer or to tell a story, then opening the book and reading in spite of the babblings of the men drying their mittens by the fire."*

biology (bi ahl′ uh je) [BIO life + LOGY study of]—the study of plant and animal life. *Biology includes botany and zoology.*

biopsy (bi′ op sē) [BIO life + OP sight]—*lit.* a seeing of live tissues; the examination of tissues removed from the living body. *The biopsy revealed that the growth was benign.*

biosphere (bi′ uh sfir)—the part of the Earth, extending from its crust out into the surrounding atmosphere, in which living things exist. *Many parts of the biosphere remain to be explored.*

symbiosis (sim bē ō sis) [SYM together + BIO life]—the living together in close union of two dissimilar organisms, often to their mutual benefit. *The symbiosis of algae and fungi forms lichens.*

symbiotic (sim bē ot′ ik) [SYM together + BIO life]—living together in a close relationship, often to the benefit of both. *In a symbiotic relationship, ants protect defenseless aphids and then "milk" them for their honeydew.*

ALSO: amphibian, antibiotic, biochemistry, bionic, microbe

✎ **EXERCISE 1**   Read each sentence and write a C in front of each sentence in which the BIO vocabulary word is used correctly. In the remaining blanks, write the word that should have been used.

1. _____ The famous actress just published her autobiography.
2. _____ Microorganisms inhabit all parts of the Earth's biosphere.
3. _____ Eve and Antwan have a symbiotic relationship: she cooks and he cleans up.
4. _____ Many people with ADHD use biology to relieve their symptoms.
5. _____ Her latest book is a biography of Raoul Wallenberg, the missing World War II hero.
6. _____ To determine whether the tumor was benign, the doctor performed a biosphere.
7. _____ Although very useful in our everyday lives, plastic is not biodegradable.
8. _____ The symbiosis of the ant and the aphid causes much distress to gardeners.

✎ **EXERCISE 2 REVIEW**   Read each sentence and write a C in front of those sentences in which the vocabulary words are used correctly. In the remaining blanks, write the word that should have been used.

1. _____ The relationship of the clownfish and the anemone is anemic.
2. _____ Through the misanthropic actions of the alumni, the college was able to offer the scholarship.
3. _____ Many companies offer bilingual customer service to their clients.
4. _____ A bivalve is a two-footed animal.
5. _____ Being ambidexterous is an advantage to a baseball player.
6. _____ My 12-year-old brother is an anomaly: he doesn't like playing video games.
7. _____ My dentist found a cavity in my bicuspid.
8. _____ Exercise is an antidote to boredom.
9. _____ The young man was assymetrical because his parents didn't enforce any rules.
10. _____ According to the annals of the college, the administration building was erected in 1920.
11. _____ The tyrannosaurus's anterior legs are shorter than its posterior legs.
12. _____ My grandmother loves to tell anecdotes from her childhood.
13. _____ The witness's ambiguous statement made me think he wasn't being straightforward.
14. _____ At 25 years old, my bicycle seems absolutely antiquarian.
15. _____ Because he died in the hospital, Bomont did not need an autopsy.

CEDE/CEED—go, yield, give away

The root SE, meaning *apart*, combines with the root CEDE, meaning *to go*, to form the word **secede**, which means to withdraw formally from an organization, alliance, political party, or federation. The U.S. Civil War began when the southern states seceded from the Union, until finally in 1991, the flag of the Soviet Union was lowered over the Kremlin for the last time, and the all-powerful Soviet Union was no more.

antecede (an' tuh sēd) [ANTE before + CEDE go]—to come, go, or exist before in time, order, rank, or position. *Pronouns substitute for nouns that antecede them.* (Antecede and precede have the same meaning.)

antecedent (an tuh sēd' unt) [ANTE before + CEDE go]—one that goes before another; also one's ancestors; and the word, phrase, or clause that determines what a pronoun refers to. *She followed in her antecedents' footsteps and became a lawyer.*

exceed (eks sēd') [EX out + CEED go]—to extend beyond or outside of. *The apple on the tree exceeds her reach.*

intercede (in' ter sēd) [INTER between + CEDE go]—to plead on another's behalf. *Daejon always intercedes in his neighbors' disputes.*

precede (prē' sēd) [PRE before + CEDE go]—to come, go, or exist before in time, order, rank, or position. *The singing of the national anthem always precedes the start of the sports event.* (Antecede and precede have the same meaning.)

precedent (prē' suh dent) [PRE before + CEDE go]—an occurrence that is used as an example in dealing with similar instances at a later time. *The Supreme Court ruling set a precedent for fair hiring practices.*

proceed (prō sēd') [PRO before + CEDE go]—to continue. *Deandra will proceed with her education despite losing her financial aid.*

recede (rē sēd') [RE back + CEDE go]—to move back or away from. *Every year he saw his hairline recede a bit more.*

retrocede (re trō' sēd) [RETRO back, behind + CEDE go]—to give back, return. *After World War II ended, Germany had to retrocede the territory it had taken during the war.*

secede (suh sēd') [SE apart + CEDE go]—to withdraw formally from membership in an organization, association, political party, or alliance. *In 1860, South Carolina was the first southern state to secede from the Union.*

succeed (suk sēd') [SUB next, after + CEED go]—to come after in time or order. *King George VI succeeded to the throne after his brother, Edward VIII, abdicated.* Also to have a favorable result. *Elaine will succeed in running the marathon since she practices regularly.*

✎ **EXERCISE 1**   Write the CEDE/CEED word next to its definition; there is one extra word.

antecede	exceed	retrocede
recede	succeed	intercede

1. _____ to move back or away from
2. _____ to have a favorable result
3. _____ to give back, return
4. _____ to plead on another's behalf
5. _____ to extend beyond or outside of

✎ **EXERCISE 2**   Write the definition next to the CEDE/CEED word.

1. antecedent _____
2. secede _____
3. recede _____
4. proceed _____
5. precedent _____

✎ **EXERCISE 3**   Write the appropriate CEDE/CEED word.

1. Georgina's miniskirt wedding dress set a _____ among her friends.
2. Four months after South Carolina _____ from the Union, six other states followed.
3. The sand _____ a bit more each year from the shore's edge.
4. The cost of the car _____ Saul's budget.
5. The directions said to _____ through two traffic lights and then turn left.

CHRON—time

Like all CHRON words, **anachronism** has something to do with *time*. It's the term applied to anything that is out of its proper historical *time*. For example, it would be an anachronism to mention antibiotics when writing about the nineteenth century.

Shakespeare let several anachronisms slip into his plays. He speaks of a clock striking in *Julius Caesar*, but striking clocks had not been invented at the time of Julius Caesar. And in *King John* he mentions using cannons, but the scenes in that play took place many years before cannons were used in England.

anachronism (un nak′ ruh niz um) [ANA back + CHRON time]—anything out of its proper historical time. *To include an electric typewriter in a story set in 1920 would be an anachronism.*

chronic (kron′ ik)—continuing for a long time, as a chronic disease. *A chronic complainer, he was never happy with his situation.*

chronicle (kron′ i kul)—an account of events arranged in order of time. The Anglo-Saxon Chronicle *gives an account of 12 centuries of British history.*

chronological (kron uh loj′ i kul)—arranged in order of time of occurrence. *The play dramatizes in chronological order the events that led to the bombing of Pearl Harbor.*

chronology (kruh nol′ uh je) [CHRON time + -LOGY study of]—a list of events arranged according to time of occurrence. *He had memorized the chronology of the reigns of the English monarchs.*

chronometer (kruh nom′ uh tur) [CHRON time + METER measure]—an instrument for measuring time precisely, especially in navigation. *Before making an entry in the log, the captain consulted the chronometer.*

synchronize (sin′ kruh nīz) [SYN together + CHRON time]—to cause to operate (keep time) in unison, as to synchronize watches or to synchronize the sound with the film in a motion picture. *The sound track of the film was not synchronized with the picture.*

✏ EXERCISE 1   Write the appropriate CHRON word.

1. The lawyer asked the witness to give a(n) ———————————— of the events.

2. Lizbeth was diagnosed with ———————————— arthritis.

3. Let's ———————————— our watches so that we don't miss the 8:12 train.

4. The ship's ———————————— was accurate to the second.

5. I find it easier to learn history when it is taught in ———————————— order.

6. With his breech pants and coonskin hat, Jared was considered a(n) ———————————— by his neighbors.

7. *The* ———————————— *of Narnia* is a series of seven fantasy novels written by C. S. Lewis.

✎ **EXERCISE 2 REVIEW**   Underline the appropriate word.

1. Her family had to listen patiently every evening to a (chronicle, chronometer) of all her achievements that day.
2. The absence of government is called (autocracy, anarchy).
3. In a (bilateral, bicameral) system of government, one legislative body acts as a check on the other.
4. They decided to spend their savings on some beautiful (antiquated, antique) furniture.
5. If Morgan continues to spend so freely, her bills will (exceed, succeed) her bank balance.
6. It would be an (ambiguity, anachronism) to describe walking on the moon in a story set in 1950.
7. His (beneficent, misanthropic) attitude toward his fellow workers made everyone dislike him.
8. The patient was trying to learn to control her autonomic nervous system through (biopsy, biofeedback).
9. After a long struggle to free itself from foreign rule, the small country finally became (autonomous, autocratic).

✎ **EXERCISE 3 REVIEW**   Give the meaning of each root and a word in which it is found.

ROOT	MEANING	WORD
1. A, AN		
2. AMBI, AMPHI		
3. ANN, ENN		
4. ANTE/ANTI		
5. ANTHROP		
6. ANTI		
7. AUTO		
8. BENE		
9. BI		
10. BIO		

CIRCUM—around

CIRCUM always means *around*. A **circumference** is the outer boundary line *around* a circular area. To **circumnavigate** the globe is to go *around* it. A **circumstance** [CIRCUM around + STA to stand] is literally something standing *around*. Perhaps the circumstance that is standing *around* and keeping you from going to a movie is a lack of money.

circuit (sur´ kit)—the regular journey around a territory by a person performing duties. *The newspaper boy made his usual circuit.* Also, a closed path followed by an electric current. *When the circuit was interrupted, the lights went out.* Also, an arrangement of electrically or electromagnetically connected components. *Computers use integrated circuits.*

circuitous (sur kyO´ uh tus)—roundabout; winding. *Because she didn't know the way, she took us by a rather circuitous route. His speech was full of circuitous arguments that led nowhere.*

circumference (sur kum´ furnts) [CIRCUM around + FER to carry]—*lit.* a line carried around; the outer boundary line around a circular area. *In our math class, we learned how to find the circumference of a circle.*

circumlocution (sur kum lō kyO´ shun) [CIRCUM around + LOC to speak]—a roundabout way of saying something. *Saying "A number of other commitments will make it impossible for me to find the time to attend the meeting" would be a circumlocution for the simple statement "I can't attend the meeting."*

circumnavigate (sur kum nav´ uh gāt) [CIRCUM around + NAV to sail]—to sail around. *Magellan was the first person to circumnavigate the globe.*

circumscribe (sur´ kum skrīb) [CIRCUM around + SCRIB to write]—*lit.* to write a line around the bounds; to limit; to confine. *The rules of the private school circumscribed the daily activities of the students.*

circumspect (sur´ kum spekt) [CIRCUM around + SPEC to look]—cautious; careful to consider possible consequences. *She was circumspect in making suggestions to her temperamental boss.*

circumstance (sur´ kum stants) [CIRCUM around + STA to stand]—*lit.* something standing around; a fact or event accompanying another fact or event. *Because of the circumstances at home, I had to give up the trip I had planned.*

circumvent (sur kum vent´) [CIRCUM around + VEN to come]—*lit.* to come around; to get around or to overcome by artful maneuvering; to prevent. *By offering a small wage increase, the management hoped to circumvent a walkout.*

✎ **EXERCISE 1 JOURNAL**   **Write three sentences in your *vocabulary journal* using CIRCUM words.**

✎ **EXERCISE 2**   Write the appropriate CIRCUM word.

1. Using _____ in your speech only confuses your listeners.
2. Magellan _____ the horn of South Africa.
3. The college's administrators plan to _____ the students' protests by raising tuition only 5 percent instead of the planned 8 percent.
4. The letter carrier's _____ took him four hours to complete.
5. Leticia's _____ attitude made her a popular manager.
6. The hikers followed a _____ path to their cabin in the woods.
7. Because of her new job, Mei's financial _____ improved greatly.
8. My mother's rules were meant to _____ our mischievous behavior.
9. The _____ of the jogging circle is exactly one mile.

✎ **EXERCISE 3 REVIEW**   Write C in front of each sentence in which all the words are used correctly. Then, in the remaining blanks, write the word that should have been used.

1. _____ The shy worker standing up and speaking at the meeting was atypical.
2. _____ I didn't really want to hear a chronological account of his day's activities.
3. _____ To bivalve the pie, cut it into two pieces.
4. _____ The Nuclear Waste Policy Act of 1982 passed with bipartisan support.
5. _____ A bicentennial celebration was held for the club's first 100 years.
6. _____ Various philanthropic organizations came to the aid of the flood victims.
7. _____ We synchronized our watches and agreed to meet at eight o'clock sharp.
8. _____ Paper containers, which are biodegradable, help keep the landscape clean.
9. _____ Pollution is causing changes in parts of the biology.
10. _____ Now that she has a job and her own apartment, Christy is autonomous.
11. _____ The per annum of D-Day is a bittersweet one for many veterans.
12. _____ The drummers synchronized their playing to achieve a thunderous effect.

✎ **EXERCISE 4**   Are you keeping up with your WORD LIST? Adding just a word or two each session will help you to increase your vocabulary.

COM, CON, COL, COR—together, with

Companion takes on new meaning when we learn its roots. A companion [COM with + PAN bread] was originally a person one shared one's bread *with*. We don't think of that original meaning today, and yet when we want to be hospitable, we invite our companions to share our food.

COM, meaning *together* or *with*, is sometimes difficult to spot because it so often changes its last letter to be like the first letter of the root following it. Thus COMloquial becomes COLloquial, COMnect becomes CONnect, and COMrelate becomes CORrelate. Sometimes the letter *m* is dropped completely, and COMeducation becomes COeducation. Changing the last letter in these ways makes pronunciation easier. On page 6 is a further discussion of changes in root spelling. Sometimes, as in **condone** and **compunction**, COM is used merely as an intensive, giving more emphasis to the root that follows.

coherent (ko hir´ unt) [CO together + HER to stick]—*lit.* sticking together; having an orderly relation of parts. *My geology professor's lectures are always coherent and interesting.*

collaborate (kuh lab´ uh rāt)—to labor together. *Two committee members are collaborating to prepare the report.*

collusion (kuh lO´ zhun) [COL together + LUD to play]—*lit.* playing together; a secret agreement between two or more persons for a deceitful purpose. *The manager suspected collusion between the two employees accused of embezzling company funds.*

commensurate (kuh men´ suh rit) [COM together + MENS to measure]—*lit.* measured together; equal in measure or size; proportionate. *The pay should be commensurate with the work.*

commiserate (kuh miz´ uh rāt) [COM with + MISERARI to pity]—to sympathize. *She commiserated with me over the loss of my job.*

commotion (kuh mo´ shun) [COM together + MOT to move]—people moving together; social disorder. *The commotion disrupted the meeting.*

complicate (kahm´ pluh kāt) [COM together + PLIC to fold]—*lit.* to fold together; to make intricate or involved. *Talking about finances will merely complicate the discussion.*

composition (kahm puh zish´ un) [COM together + POS to put]—a putting together of parts to form a whole. *I was finally satisfied with the composition I had written.*

compunction (kum pungk´ shun) [COM (intensive) + PUNCT to prick]—*lit.* a prick of conscience; an uneasiness caused by a sense of guilt; a slight regret. *He felt some compunction about taking so much of his tutor's time.*

condone (kun don´) [COM (intensive) + DON to give]—to forgive or overlook (an offense). *The public can't condone the dishonest dealings of the company representative.*

congenital (kun jen´ uh tul) [CON together + GEN birth]—*lit.* born together; existing at birth. *The child has a congenital heart defect.*

consensus (kun sen´ sus) [CON together + SENS to feel]—*lit.* a feeling together; general agreement. *No consensus has been reached about the safety of nuclear plants.*

consummate (kun sum´ it) [CON together + SUMMA sum]—*lit.* summed up together; complete or perfect in every respect. *She was a consummate artist.* Also, complete; utter, as a consummate bore.

contemporary (kun tem′ puh rer ē) [CON together + TEMPOR time]—*lit.* together in time; belonging to the same age. *We're studying some contemporary novelists as well as those from the past.*

convene (kun ven′) [CON together + VEN to come]—to come together formally. *The committee will convene next week.*

convivial (kun viv′ ē ul) [CON together + VIV to live]—fond of eating, drinking, and being sociable together. *In a convivial mood, the guests stayed until midnight.*

correlate (kor′ uh lāt)—to relate together; to show relationship. *The accountant is trying to correlate this year's figures with last year's.*

ALSO: colloquial, colloquium, complacent, compulsive, concoction, concord, concourse, concur, concurrent, conducive, congregation, conjugal, conscription, conversant, corrupt

EXERCISE 1   **Choose the appropriate COM, CON, COL, or COR word to fill in the blank in each sentence.**

coherent	consummate	convivial	contemporary
collaborated	collusion	condone	composition
commotion	complicated		

1. The drunkard's rambling explanation was not _____.
2. The warden realized that the guard was in _____ with the inmate.
3. The _____ of the furniture, paint, and rug was visually pleasing.
4. He is the _____ butler, down to his English accent.
5. The child's running around caused a _____ at the restaurant.
6. The Windsor Book Club is a _____ group whose meetings are well attended.
7. The chairman's anecdote only _____ the explanation.
8. The artist and the writer _____ on the Web site's visuals and content.
9. Refusing to _____ her son's rude behavior, the mother sent him to time out.
10. He prefers country decor to _____ furnishings.

EXERCISE 2   Write the appropriate COM, CON, COL, or COR word.

1. His rate of promotion is not _____ with his hard work.

2. The manager does not _____ his sloppy work.

3. Her IQ score and her grades did not _____.

4. I felt no _____ about missing that meeting.

5. None of her friends were available to _____ with her about her losing her job.

6. The _____ of the committee was that more funds were necessary to support the school's athletic programs.

7. The two students will _____ on the science project.

8. The child's inability to hear was traced to a _____ defect.

9. Upset, the driver was unable to give a _____ account of the accident.

10. The board members will break for lunch and _____ again at two.

EXERCISE 3 JOURNAL   In your *vocabulary journal,* write a few sentences describing a party. Use as many of your COM, CON, COL, or COR vocabulary words as possible.

COM, CON, COL, COR—together, with **41**

✎ **EXERCISE 4 REVIEW**   Using the following nine words, fill in the blanks in the paragraph so that it makes sense. After you check your answers in the back of the book, reread the paragraph and see how satisfying it is to read a paragraph in which you are sure of all the words.

biodegradable	circuitous	biology
amphibians	compunction	condone
perennial	bivalves	ambivalent

Last weekend our _____ class went to the lake to study _____, _____, and various other forms of marine life. On our way there, we took a _____ route through a wooded area and were dismayed to find the roadside cluttered with bottles, plastic cartons, and other trash that isn't _____. People seem _____ about our natural scenery. They like a beautiful countryside, yet they litter. They wouldn't _____ messiness in their own backyards, yet they feel no _____ about tossing a bottle or candy wrapper into the woods. It is a _____ problem, and it will be solved only when each individual develops a responsible attitude toward our natural scenery.

CRED—to believe

In the Middle Ages, it was customary for servants to carry the prepared food from the kitchen to a small side table in the dining hall, where, in front of the master and his guests, one of the servants would taste the food to show that it was not spoiled or poisoned. This side table came to be called a credence (belief or trust), and today in France, a side table is still called a *crédence* and in Italy a *credenza*. Today in the U.S., a side table is sometimes called a *credenza*. Our English word **credence** no longer refers to our trust in the food we eat, but we still speak of having credence (belief or trust) in what we read and in what people tell us.

Note how the following CRED words go in pairs:

credible—believable
incredible—unbelievable

credulous—believing too readily
incredulous—not believing readily

credulity—tendency to believe readily
incredulity—tendency not to believe readily

credence (kre´ duns)—belief; acceptance as true. *They should not have given any credence to the rumor.*

credentials (kri den´ shuls)—documents that cause others to believe in one. *The credentials she brought from her last job were excellent.*

credibility (kred uh bil´ uh tē)—trustworthiness. *No one ever questioned his credibility.*

credible (kred´ uh bul)—believable. *He gave a credible explanation for his tardiness.*

credit (kred´ ut)—trust, as financial credit; a source of honor, as a credit to one's family. *She always paid cash rather than asking for credit.*

credulity (kri dO´ li tē)—tendency to believe readily on too little evidence; gullibility. *Her credulity made her easy prey for anyone with a hard luck story.*

credulous (krej´ uh lus)—believing too readily on too little evidence; gullible. *Only a credulous person would be taken in by such ads.*

creed (krēd)—a formal statement of religious or other belief, as the creed of a church. *She learned to repeat the Apostles' Creed.*

discredit (dis kred´ ut) [DIS not + CRED to believe]—lit. not to believe; to distrust; to destroy belief in. *Because the newspaper articles had discredited the mayor, he resigned.*

incredible (in kred´ uh bul) [IN not + CRED to believe]—unbelievable. *The amount of work she could do in an hour was incredible.*

incredulity (in kri dO´ li tē) [IN not + CRED to believe]—tendency not to believe readily; skepticism. *As he listened to their excuses, his incredulity was obvious.*

incredulous (in krej´ uh lus) [IN not + CRED to believe]—not believing readily; disbelieving. *When she heard she had won the prize, she was incredulous.*

miscreant (mis´ krē unt) [MIS less + CRED to believe]—originally, an unbeliever in religion; now, an evildoer or criminal. *The police were trying to round up the miscreants.*

ALSO: accreditation, accredited, creditor

✎ **EXERCISE 1**   Write the appropriate CRED word.

1. When they learned that their son had eloped, they were _____.
2. On his two-week trek through the woods, he had some _____ adventures, including avoiding a bear.
3. The _____ has so far evaded the police.
4. The excuse he gave was simply not _____.
5. His spending habits have marked him as a poor _____ risk.
6. He had to produce _____ before he was allowed to enter the laboratory.
7. The defense attorney knew they'd lost when the jury treated his client's alibi with _____.
8. I wouldn't give any _____ to such a poorly documented story.
9. The jury questioned the _____ of the witness.
10. I'm not so _____ as to believe all I am told.

✎ **EXERCISE 2**   Match each CRED word with its definition.

A. creed   **C.** credence   **E.** incredulous
B. credulous   **D.** incredible   **F.** miscreant

1. _____ unbelievable
2. _____ believing too readily
3. _____ not believing readily
4. _____ acceptance as true
5. _____ a declaration of one's religious or other belief
6. _____ an evildoer or criminal

✎ **EXERCISE 3**   Underline the appropriate CRED word.

1. Because her (credit, creed) was excellent, the bank manager approved her loan.
2. The fans reacted with (credible, incredulity) at the umpire's calls.
3. The visiting lecturer's (miscreant, credentials) are top-notch.
4. His history of lies led the dean of students to (discredit, credit) his story.
5. Her personal (creed, credence) of fairness and honesty has served her well throughout her life.

CUR—to run

If you find it difficult to hang on to your money, don't be surprised—the word **currency** means literally *running*. The currency in circulation in a country is constantly *running* from person to person. And if currency should *run* through the hands of a person or a company too rapidly, it might be the **precursor** [PRE before + CUR to run] or forerunner of bankruptcy.

concourse (kon´ kors) [CON together + CUR to run]—*lit.* a running together; a large open space where crowds gather. *The main concourse in the airport was filled with tourists.*

concur (kon kur´) [CON together + CUR to run]—*lit.* to run together; to agree. *We all concur with the recommendation of the committee.*

concurrent (kun kur´ unt) [CON together + CUR to run]—*lit.* running together; occurring at the same time. *The town council and the school board held concurrent meetings.*

courier (kur´ ē ur) [CUR to run]—one who carries (runs with) messages. *The courier arrived with the letter.*

course (kors´) [CUR to run]—a running onward from one point to the next, as the course of a stream; in education, a series of studies leading (running) toward a degree. *I like all the courses required for my major.*

currency (kur´ un sē) [CUR to run]—money that passes (runs) from person to person in a country. *The currency in that country is mostly silver.*

current (kur´ unt) [CUR to run]—the flow (running) of water, air, or electricity; prevalent at the moment (running along), as current fashions. *The current trend is toward smaller cars.*

curriculum (kuh rik´ yuh lum) [CUR to run]—originally, a race course; today, all the courses offered by an educational institution. *The curriculum offers me a wide choice of courses.*

cursive (kur´ siv) [CUR to run]—*lit.* running along; handwriting with the letters joined together. *She preferred to print rather than write in cursive.*

cursory (kur´ suh re)—running over rapidly without attention to detail; hasty and superficial. *She gave the novel only a cursory reading.*

discourse (dis´ kors) [DIS apart + CUR to run]—*lit.* to run about; to speak at length; a formal and lengthy discussion of a subject. *He gave a discourse on Ibsen's symbolism.*

excursion (ik skur´ zhun) [EX out + CUR to run]—*lit.* a running out somewhere; a short journey. *We took a day's excursion down the river.*

occur (uh kur´) [OB toward + CUR to run]—*lit.* to run toward; to take place; to happen. *I was amazed at what had occurred.*

precursor (pri kur´ sur) [PRE before + CUR to run]—a person or thing that runs before; a forerunner. *The fountain pen was the precursor of the ballpoint.*

recourse (re´ kors) [RE back + CUR to run]—*lit.* a running back (for help); a turning to someone or something for help. *His only recourse was to notify the police.*

recur (ri kur´) [RE again + CUR to run]—*lit.* to run again; to happen again. *If the problem should recur, you'll have to buy a new battery.*

recurrent (ri kur´ unt) [RE back + CUR to run]—*lit.* running back; returning repeatedly. *They still had the recurrent problem of absenteeism.*

ALSO: concurrence, corridor, incur, incursion, occurrence

✎ EXERCISE 1   Match each word with its definition.

A. precursor   *C.* curriculum   **E.** cursive
B. courier   **D.** recur   **F.** discourse

1. _____ the courses offered by an educational institution
2. _____ handwriting with the letters joined together
3. _____ a forerunner
4. _____ to speak at length
5. _____ one who carries messages
6. _____ to happen again

✎ EXERCISE 2   Write the appropriate CUR word.

1. Because the two parties were _____, Stan had to choose which one to attend.
2. Her day-long _____ to the mountains made her feel as if she had vacationed for a week.
3. When we landed in England, we exchanged our American _____ for British pounds.
4. The swift _____ carried our raft down the river.
5. Most colleges include a core _____ of English, math, and science.
6. The marathon runners' _____ took them through the city's scenic parks.
7. His _____ attacks of asthma convinced him to see a specialist.
8. I _____ with your suggestions and will recommend them to the group.
9. I was surprised at his _____ reading of the important legal document.
10. Hundreds of waiting passengers filled the airport's _____.

✎ EXERCISE 3   In your *vocabulary journal,* write four sentences about a track-and-field meet. Use as many of your CUR vocabulary words as possible.

DEM—people

Many words have changed their meanings over the centuries, some having changed so much that they now mean almost the opposite of what they meant originally. **Demagogue** is an example.

First used at the time of the Peloponnesian War, the word demagogue (DEM people + AGOG leader) referred to a leader or orator who championed the cause of the common *people* of Athens in their fight against the aristocrats of Sparta. Gradually through the years, however, such leaders began pursuing their own interests rather than helping the people, and today a demagogue is a political leader who makes impassioned appeals to the emotions and prejudices of *people* to gain personal power.

demagogue (dem´ uh gog) [DEM people + AGOG leader]—originally, a leader of the common people; now, a leader who stirs up the people by appealing to their emotions and prejudices to win them over quickly and thus gain power. *Interested only in gaining personal power, the candidate was a demagogue.*

demagoguery (dem´ uh gog uh re) [DEM people + AGOG leader]—the methods or practices of a demagogue. *Her campaign speech was pure demagoguery.*

democracy (di mahk´ ru sē) [DEM people + CRAC to rule]—*lit.* people rule; government by representatives elected by the people. *More countries are now choosing democracy.*

demographic (dem uh graf´ ik) [DEM people + GRAPH to write]—*lit.* writing about people; pertaining to the study of human populations, especially their density, distribution, and vital statistics. *The 2000 census gathered a wealth of demographic information.*

endemic (en dem´ ik) [EN in + DEM people]—native to a particular people or country, as an endemic disease, which occurs only among certain people, or an endemic plant or animal, which is found only in a certain location. *The snail darter, an endangered species, is endemic to the Little Tennessee River.*

epidemic (ep uh dem´ ik) [EPI upon + DEM people]—*lit.* upon the people; a disease or other abnormal condition spreading rapidly among many people. *The flu epidemic caused many absences from work.*

pandemic (pan dem´ ik) [PAN all + DEM people]—*lit.* among all the people; widespread. *The economic depression was pandemic.*

ALSO: democrat, democratic, demography

✎ EXERCISE 1 JOURNAL   Write several sentences in your *vocabulary journal* using some of the CRED, CUR, and DEM words you have learned. Check the sentence given in the explanation of each word to make sure you are using the word correctly.

✏️ **EXERCISE 2**   Write the appropriate DEM word.

1. There was great fear that this strain of flu would become _____.
2. Because of the vaccination program, the citizens no longer fear a smallpox _____.
3. _____ information is essential to choosing a business location.
4. The newly formed government was proud to be a _____.
5. The eucalyptus tree is _____ to Australia, but now it can be found in many parts of the world.
6. The mayor is a _____, seeking only to advance his own career.

✏️ **EXERCISE 3 REVIEW**   Give the meaning of each root and a word in which it is found.

ROOT	MEANING	WORD
1. A, AN	_____	_____
2. AMBI, AMPHI	_____	_____
3. ANN, ENN	_____	_____
4. ANTE, ANTI	_____	_____
5. ANTHROP	_____	_____
6. ANTI	_____	_____
7. AUTO	_____	_____
8. BENE	_____	_____
9. BI	_____	_____
10. BIO	_____	_____
11. CEDE, CEED	_____	_____
12. CHRON	_____	_____
13. CIRCUM	_____	_____
14. COM, CON, COL, COR	_____	_____
15. CRED	_____	_____
16. CUR	_____	_____

DICT—to speak

The word **addict** has had a long history. In Roman law, to addict a person meant to turn that person over to a master by sentence *(speaking)* of the court. Through the years, addict has kept something of its old meaning in that it now refers to turning oneself over to a habit, which can, of course, be a master.

abdicate (ab´ di kāt) [AB away + DICT to speak, proclaim]—*lit.* to proclaim away; to renounce formally a throne or high office. *The king abdicated.*

addict (uh dikt´) [AD to + DICT to speak]—*lit.* to speak to or to sentence oneself; to give oneself habitually or compulsively to something. *He was addicted to alcohol.*

contradict (kahn tru dikt´) [CONTRA against + DICT to speak]—to speak against; to assert the opposite of what someone has said. *I didn't dare contradict her.*

dictate (dik´ tāt)—to speak or read something aloud to be recorded by another; to give (speak) orders or commands. *The boss dictates his letters slowly.*

dictator (dik´ tāt ur)—one whose speech is to be taken as the final word; one who orders others around; a tyrannical ruler. *The small country was ruled by a dictator.*

dictatorial (dik tu tor´ ē ul)—speaking and acting in a domineering or oppressive way. *The crew resented the dictatorial manner of the foreman.*

diction (dik´ shun)—choice of words in speaking or writing. *She used excellent diction, always choosing exactly the right word.* Also, enunciation in speaking or singing. *His diction was so clear that he could be understood at the back of the auditorium.*

dictionary (dik´ shu ner ē)—a book containing the words of a (spoken) language. *I'd be lost without my dictionary.*

edict (ē´ dikt) [E out + DICT to speak]—*lit.* a speaking out; an official decree. *The Edict of Nantes granted toleration to Protestants in France.*

jurisdiction (joor us dik´ shun) [JURIS law + DICT to speak]—the right to interpret (speak) and apply the law; legal power to hear and decide cases; the extent of such judicial or other authority. *The case was not within the court's jurisdiction.*

predict (pri dikt´) [PRE before + DICT to speak]—*lit.* to speak beforehand; to foretell. *The Bureau of Meteorology is predicting a late spring.*

valedictorian (val uh dik tor´ ē un) [VALE farewell + DICT to speak]—a student, usually of the highest scholastic standing, who gives the farewell speech at commencement. *As valedictorian of her class, she gave a good speech at graduation.*

ALSO: addiction, benediction, dictum, ditto, interdict, malediction, verdict

EXERCISE 1 JOURNAL   In your *vocabulary journal,* write a few sentences using your DICT words. Pick the ones you are unfamiliar with.

✎ **EXERCISE 2**   Write the appropriate DICT word.

1. When Edward VII _____ his throne to marry Mrs. Simpson, the world was shocked.
2. The manager _____ his resignation letter to his secretary.
3. The large number of cases in her _____ overwhelmed the judge.
4. Because she has the highest grade point average, she is the _____ of her class.
5. My mother jokes that she is a chocolate _____ since she eats some after each meal.
6. The foreign student took classes to improve his _____.
7. The teacher was _____, never allowing her students to voice their opinions.
8. Based on her improved study habits, Sharmilla _____ a successful semester.
9. The king's _____ granted all citizens the right to own property.
10. If I want to know about a word, I look it up in my _____.
11. The evidence will either affirm or _____ his story.

✎ **EXERCISE 3 REVIEW**   Which word names or describes the following?

1. a marriage to a person while legally married to another _____
2. a study of the cultural development of human beings _____
3. someone who benefits from a gift or a will _____
4. a two-footed animal _____
5. without moral standards _____
6. anything out of its proper historical time _____
7. belief; acceptance as true _____
8. secret agreement for a deceitful purpose _____
9. cautious; careful to consider possible consequences _____
10. continuing for a long time _____

✎ **EXERCISE 4**   Are you adding words to your WORD LIST at the end of this book?

DIS, DI, DIF—not, away, apart

It was important in Roman times to start a journey or begin a new venture on a lucky day. One way to find out whether a day was favorable was to consult the stars. If the stars were *not* in a favorable position, the outcome of any undertaking begun on that day was certain to be a **disaster** (DIS not + ASTER star).

disarray (dis uh rā´) [DIS not + AREER to array]—*lit.* not arrayed or arranged properly; a state of disorder or confusion; disorderly dress. *Following the death of their leader, the political group fell into disarray.*

disburse (dis burs´) [DIS away + BURSA a purse]—*lit.* to take away from a purse; to pay out, as from a fund. *The president of the society disbursed the scholarship funds.*

discomfit (dis kum´ fit) [DIS not + COM together + FAC to do]—*lit.* to undo; to thwart the plans of; to make uneasy. *The leader felt discomfited because his motives were being questioned.*

disconcert (dis kun surt´) [DIS not + CONCERT to bring into agreement]—to upset; to frustrate. *The speaker was disconcerted by the noise in the balcony.* (Disconcert and discomfit are close synonyms.)

disconsolate (dis kon´ suh lit)—not able to be consoled; hopelessly sad. *The team member responsible for losing the relay was disconsolate.*

discordant (dis kor´ dunt) [DIS apart + CORD heart]—*lit.* hearts apart; not in accord; disagreeable to the ear. *One discordant voice can ruin a choir.*

dismantle (dis mant´ ul) [DIS apart + MANTEL cloak]—originally, to take a man's cloak off his back; to strip a house of furnishings; to take apart. *I dismantled the room for the painters.*

disparate (dis par´ ut) [DIS not + PAR equal]—*lit.* not equal; unlike. *The reporter wrote on subjects as disparate as ice hockey and women's fashions.*

disparity (di spar´ uh tē) [DIS not + PAR equal]—difference; unlikeness. *In spite of the disparity in their ages, they get along well.*

disproportionate (dis pruh por´ shun it)—not proportionate; out of proportion in size, shape, or amount. *His salary was disproportionate to the amount of work he did.*

dissect (dis ekt´) [DIS apart + SECT to cut]—to cut apart, especially for anatomical study. *Our class dissected frogs yesterday.*

disseminate (di sem´ uh nāt) [DIS apart + SEMIN seed]—to spread abroad as if sowing seed. *The publication disseminated information about endangered species.*

dissent (di sent´) [DIS apart + SENT to feel]—to differ in opinion or feeling; to withhold approval. *If too many members dissent, the motion will not pass.*

dissident (dis´ uh dunt) [DIS apart + SID to sit]—*lit.* sitting apart; one who disagrees; a dissenter. *The dissidents made trouble for the ruling party.*

dissuade (di swād´) [DIS away + SUAD to persuade]—to turn a person away (from a course) by persuasion. *Finally they dissuaded him from giving up his job.*

diverse (di vurs´) [DI away + VERS to turn]—*lit.* turned away from each other; unlike, as diverse opinions. *The committee listened to all the diverse views.*

diversion (duh vur´ zyun) [DI away + VERS to turn]—something that turns the mind away and relaxes or entertains. *Her favorite diversion is golf.*

ALSO: diffident, diffuse, discord, discourse, discredit, discrepancy, discursive, dismiss, disparage, dispel, dispense, disrupt, dissolution, dissonant, distort, diversity, divert

EXERCISE 1   Write the appropriate DIS, DI, DIF word.

1. Kathy woke up, looked at the time, and sped out the door, her hair and clothes in
   _____ .

2. George will _____ the car's engine before starting to rebuild it.

3. The bride and groom are from such _____ backgrounds that many
   wondered how they became a couple.

4. To _____ the information about its new campus, the college took
   out newspaper and radio advertisements.

5. Her _____ singing kept the carolers from enjoying the evening.

6. The _____ between what she expected for her birthday and what
   she received was enormous.

7. The club members agreed on how to _____ their funds.

8. To gain a broad background, the student enrolled in a _____
   curriculum.

9. The lone _____ was ignored during the budget meeting.

10. Leaders of the D.A.R.E. program hope to _____ youngsters from
    using illegal drugs.

EXERCISE 2   Match each word with its definition.

A. dissect	**C.** discomfit	**E.** disproportionate
B. diversion	**D.** dissent	**F.** disconsolate

1. _____ to make uneasy
2. _____ something that turns the mind away and relaxes or entertains
3. _____ not able to be consoled
4. _____ to withhold approval
5. _____ to cut apart
6. _____ out of proportion in size, shape, or amount

EXERCISE 3 REVIEW   What word names or describes each of the following?

1. occurring two times a year _____

2. trustworthiness _____

3. having a desire to succeed _____

4. all the courses offered by an academic institution _____

5. native to a particular people _____

6. to speak at length _____

7. to make intricate or involved _____

8. an account of events arranged in order of time _____

9. a short journey _____

10. occurring at the same time _____

EXERCISE 4 JOURNAL   In your *vocabulary journal,* write three sentences about a lecture that you have attended. You may use any of the words you have studied so far.

✎ **EXERCISE 5 REVIEW**   Fill in the root and its meaning for each word. Some roots are used more than once.

WORD	ROOT	MEANING
1. asymmetrical		
2. ambiguity		
3. autocrat		
4. biology		
5. circumvent		
6. credible		
7. demographic		
8. disparity		
9. biannual		
10. synchronize		
11. collusion		
12. courier		
13. jurisdiction		
14. dismantle		
15. semiannual		
16. anterior		
17. anthropology		
18. antithesis		
19. benign		
20. bisect		
21. chronicle		
22. compunction		
23. exceed		
24. current		
25. anomaly		

EQU—equal

If you're looking for a climate that's *equally* pleasant in summer and winter, you're looking for an **equable** climate. If you're eager for spring, you're waiting for the spring **equinox**, when days and nights are *equal*. If you want a fair settlement of a legal case, you want an **equitable** settlement. And if you can remain *equally* calm and composed under pleasant or unpleasant circumstances, you're able to maintain your **equanimity**.

adequate (ad' i kwut) [AD to + EQU equal]—equal to what is required; sufficient. *I was sure my preparation for that exam was adequate.*

equable (ek' wuh bul)—equal at all times; unvarying. *Hawaii has an equable climate, equally pleasant in summer and winter.*

equanimity (e kwuh nim' uh tē) [EQU equal + ANIM mind]—evenness of mind or temper; composure. *No matter what happened, she always maintained her equanimity.*

equate (i kwāt)—to represent as equal. *It's not possible to equate money and happiness.*

equator (i kwat' ur)—a line equally distant at all points from the North and South Poles. *The ship sailed across the equator at noon.*

equilateral (ē kwuh lat' ur ul) [EQU equal + LATER side]—having equal sides. *He drew an equilateral triangle on the board.*

equilibrium (ē kwuh lib' re um) [EQU equal + LIBR balance]—a state of balance. *When the horse swerved, the boy lost his equilibrium and fell off.*

equinox (ē' kwuh noks) [EQU equal + NOX night]—*lit.* equal night; the time of year when the sun crosses the equator and day and night are of equal length. *The spring equinox on March 21 marks the beginning of spring.*

equitable (ek' wuh tuh bul)—reasonable; fair; just. *They achieved an equitable settlement out of court.*

equity (ek' wuh tē)—an ownership right to property. *Because they had paid so little on the mortgage, they had little equity in the house.*

equivalent (i kwiv' u lunt)—equal in value, force, or meaning. *The prize was equivalent to a month's wages.*

equivocal (i kwiv' uh kul) [EQU equal + VOC voice]—*lit.* having equal voices; capable of two interpretations. *Her equivocal reply was so carefully worded that the members of each faction thought she favored them.*

equivocate (i kwiv' uh kāt) [EQU equal + VOC voice]—*lit.* to use equal voices; to make statements with two possible meanings in order to mislead. *The candidate equivocated so much that it was impossible to tell where he stood on any issue.*

ALSO: equalize, equation, equidistant, inadequate, inequality, inequity, iniquity, unequivocal

✎ **EXERCISE 1**   Write the appropriate EQU word.

1. It's not always possible to _____ salary and job satisfaction.
2. Because he has so often _____, people are reluctant to believe him.
3. Having paid off the mortgage, we now have full _____ in our house.
4. His _____ in times of crisis was amazing.
5. While trying to ride on my bike with several packages, I lost my _____.
6. Florida has a more _____ climate than Maine.
7. After the fall _____, the days get shorter.
8. The shape of the island was roughly that of an _____ triangle.
9. In giving an _____ answer, he tried to please everyone but actually pleased no one.
10. An _____ agreement was finally reached by the contractor and the builder.
11. The amount of lumber was _____ for the project.
12. According to the grading sheet, a score of 85 is _____ to a grade of "B."
13. The trip to the _____ took two days by boat.

✎ **EXERCISE 2 REVIEW**   Write C in front of each sentence in which all words are used correctly.

1. _____ Radio and television make it easy to disseminate information.
2. _____ Her excuse was so credible that no one believed her.
3. _____ It usually is possible to correlate vocabulary and success in college.
4. _____ They had a symbiotic relationship, each working better when they worked together.
5. _____ The judge's lenient sentence set a precedent for the way that crime was treated in court.
6. _____ A miscreant is an error in a term paper.
7. _____ A bilateral agreement is written in two languages.
8. _____ Coherent speech is orderly and easy to follow.
9. _____ An amphibious animal can live both on land and in the water.
10. _____ As an atheist, he attended church services each morning.

EU—good, well

If you are in a state of **euphoria**, you feel that life is *good*, that everything is going *well*. EU always means *good* or *well*. A **eulogy** is a speech that says *good* things about someone; **euphonious** prose has a pleasant *(good)* sound; and the controversial subject of **euthanasia** is concerned literally with a *good* death, a death for merciful reasons.

Do you ever use **euphemisms**? Look under *euphemism* in the following list and find out.

eulogize (yO´ luh jiz) [EU good + LOG speech]—*lit.* to give a good speech; to give a speech in praise of. *The man who had started the project was eulogized by all the speakers.*

eulogy (yO´ luh je) [EU good + LOG speech]—*lit.* a good speech; spoken or written praise of someone or something, especially praise of a person who has recently died. *He gave a moving eulogy at the funeral of his friend.*

euphemism (yO´ fuh miz um)—the substitution of a mild (good) word in place of a distasteful or unpleasant one. *She spoke in euphemisms, talking of passing on rather than dying, of the departed rather than the dead, and of the underprivileged rather than the poor.*

euphonious (yO fo´ nē us) [EU good + PHON sound]—having a pleasant (good) sound; harmonious. *I listened to the euphonious sounds of the forest.*

euphony (yO´ fuh nē) [EU good + PHON sound]—*lit.* good sound; a harmonious succession of words having a pleasing sound. *I like the euphony of the speeches of Martin Luther King, Jr.*

euphoria (yO for´ ē uh)—a feeling of well-being. *After she became engaged, she was in a state of euphoria.*

euthanasia (yO thuh nā´ zhuh) [EU good + THAN death]—*lit.* a good death; painless putting to death for merciful reasons, as with a terminal illness. *They advocated a law permitting euthanasia for those who are suffering and will not get well.*

ALSO: eucalyptus, Eugene, eugenics

EXERCISE 1   Match the EU word with its definition. There is one extra definition.

A. eulogize   **B.** eulogy   **C.** euphemism   **D.** euphonious

E. euphony   **F.** euphoria   **G.** euthanasia

1. a feeling of well-being _____

2. having a pleasant sound _____

3. to give a speech in praise of _____

4. painless putting to death for merciful reasons _____

5. substitution of a mild word in place of a distasteful one _____

✎ **EXERCISE 2**   Write the appropriate EU word.

1. In Denmark, _____ is legal for the terminally ill.
2. Aaron's piano playing was _____ to his teacher's ears.
3. Anthony's _____ after the death of Julius Caesar is one of the best-known passages in Shakespeare's writing.
4. After earning an A+ on her report, Diane was in a state of _____.
5. The philanthropist was _____ for his charitable work.
6. The _____ of nursery rhymes is soothing to babies.
7. Rather than speak bluntly, she used _____ to convey her meaning.

✎ **EXERCISE 3 REVIEW**   Write a C in front of each sentence in which all words are used correctly.

1. _____ To circumvent is to open all the windows.
2. _____ Many children's books have anthropomorphic characters.
3. _____ Her explanation, full of circumlocutions, never did get to the point.
4. _____ The speaker's long discourse on dieting was boring.
5. _____ A convivial group gathered for the holiday celebration.
6. _____ My friend and I collaborated to design the poster.
7. _____ The supervisor went around to circumspect each employee's work.
8. _____ A companion was originally a person with whom one shared bread.
9. _____ The father is an autocrat; the rest of the family bows to his wishes.
10. _____ A credulous person tends to believe without sufficient evidence.
11. _____ The tremendous amount of work he did was disproportionate to his small salary.
12. _____ A consensus is the recording of the population in an area.
13. _____ The music teacher was pleased with the euphonious playing of her students.
14. _____ Realizing he was outmatched, the chess player ceded the game.
15. _____ My reading teacher taught us to predict the ending of the story.

✎ **EXERCISE 3 JOURNAL**   Write several sentences in your *vocabulary journal* using words from the EQU and EU sections. Be sure the sentences show the words' meaning.

EX, ES, E—out

Our word **escape** means breaking loose from any confinement, but originally it had a more picturesque meaning. In Roman times, perhaps when a jailor was trying to hang on to a prisoner by his cape, the prisoner slipped *out* of his cape and left it in the hands of the jailor: The prisoner had escaped (ES out + CAP cape). He had got "out of his cape" and gone free.

ebullient (i bŏl′ yunt) [E out + BULL to bubble or boil]—bubbling out; overflowing with enthusiasm. *Her ebullient manner made her an entertaining lecturer.*

educate (ej′ uh kāt) [E out + DUC to lead]—*lit.* to lead out (draw out) the inborn abilities of a pupil; to develop or train. *I'm trying to educate my puppy.*

efface (i fās′) [E out + FAC face]—*lit.* to remove the face of; to wipe out. *Nothing could efface the memory of that storm.*

emigrate (em′ uh grāt) [E out + MIGRA to move]—to move out of a country (in contrast to immigrate, which means to move into a country). *My ancestors emigrated from Germany.*

emit (ē mit′) [E out + MIT to send]—to send out, as a child emits a scream or a factory emits smoke. *The boy emitted a yell as he reached the goal.*

emolument (i mol′ yuh munt) [E out + MOL to grind]—originally a miller's fee for grinding (out) grain; now, a payment for services rendered. *Even though she received no emolument, she liked doing the job.*

enervate (en′ ur vāt) [E out + NERV nerve]—*lit.* to take out the nerve; to deprive of nerve, force, vigor; to weaken. *She found the hot, humid climate enervating.*

eradicate (i rad′ i kāt) [E out + RADIC root]—*lit.* to tear out by the roots; to destroy. *It's difficult to eradicate racial prejudice.*

excavate (ek′ skuh vāt) [EX out + CAV hollow]—to hollow out, to dig out and remove. *They were excavating some ancient dinosaur bones.*

excoriate (ek skor′ e āt) [EX out + COR skin]—*lit.* to strip the skin off; to denounce harshly. *The candidate excoriated his opponent, lashing out at him in his public speeches.*

exonerate (eg zon′ uh rāt) [EX out + ONER burden]—*lit.* to take the burden out; to free from a charge or from guilt. *The jury exonerated him.*

expatiate (ek spā shē āt) [EX out + SPATIUM space, course]—*lit.* to wander out of the course; to digress; to speak or write at length. *The salesperson expatiated on the value of the product until everyone was bored.*

expatriate (eks pāt′ rē ut) [EX out + PATRIA native country]—one who has left one's country or renounced allegiance to it. *She was an expatriate from Germany.*

export (ek sport′) [EX out + PORT to carry]—to carry out of a country. *Some countries in the tropics export bananas.*

expurgate (eks′ pur gāt) [EX out + PURG to clean]—*lit.* to clean out; to take out obscene or objectionable material. *The cast voted to expurgate a shocking scene from the play.*

exterminate (ek stur′ muh nāt) [EX out + TERMINUS boundary]—*lit.* to put things out of the boundary; to destroy living things by killing off all individuals. *I'm trying to exterminate these cockroaches.*

(Exterminate and eradicate are nearly synonymous. Exterminate means to destroy utterly and is applied to insects or people. Eradicate implies an uprooting and is applied to a disease, a fault, or a prejudice.)

ALSO: edict, effusive, egregious, eloquent, elucidate, eject, emissary, erase, erupt, escape, eventuate, evoke, exacerbate, exclaim, excise, exclude, exculpate, exodus, expedite, expel, extort

✎ EXERCISE 1 Write the appropriate EX, ES, E word.

1. The accused was certain the evidence would _____ him.
2. The editor _____ the offensive language from the novel.
3. During World War II, Nazis used the euphemism "_____" for the murder of Jews.
4. With more research, AIDS may someday be _____.
5. She _____ about her ailments until our eyes glazed over.
6. The angry speaker _____ anyone who disagreed with him.
7. The kindergarten teacher's lively, _____ personality made the children love her.
8. The volunteers expected no _____ for their services.
9. The archeologist will _____ the Mayan site after he confirms his funding.
10. The English poet Lord Byron was an _____ in Italy.

✎ EXERCISE 2 Match each word with its definition.

A. emit	**D.** expatiate	**G.** enervate
B. excoriate	**E.** eradicate	**H.** export
C. ebullient	**F.** excavate	

1. _____ to send out of a country
2. _____ to send out
3. _____ to destroy
4. _____ to denounce harshly
5. _____ to hollow out; to dig out and remove
6. _____ to digress; to speak or write at length
7. _____ overflowing with enthusiasm
8. _____ to weaken

EXERCISE 3 REVIEW   Write C in front of each sentence in which all the words are used correctly.

1. _____ She commiserated with me when I lost my job.

2. _____ His wild tales strain my incredulity.

3. _____ She's a consummate decorator, designing the finest interiors in the city.

4. _____ The committee decided to convene after lunch.

5. _____ Her recurrent absences are giving her a bad reputation.

6. _____ The edict of the president left no room for argument.

7. _____ Our supervisor gets good results without being dictatorial.

8. _____ The Constitution speaks of the equality of opportunity in our country.

9. _____ She abdicated the throne in favor of her son.

10. _____ His attack of symbiosis was mild, and he soon recovered.

11. _____ The disease had become pandemic, afflicting many nations.

12. _____ A biopsy is the examination of tissue taken from a living person, whereas an autopsy is the examination of a dead person.

13. _____ Since he is ambidextrous, his broken arm didn't stop him from taking notes in class.

14. _____ Because she was an amphibian about the institution of marriage, she broke off her engagement.

15. _____ The United States celebrated its biennial in 1876.

EXERCISE 4 JOURNAL   In your *vocabulary journal,* write a few sentences describing some people you know. Use as many of your EX, ES, and E vocabulary words as possible.

✎ **EXERCISE 5 REVIEW**   Give the meaning of each root and a word in which it is found.

ROOT	MEANING	WORD
1. A, AN		
2. AMBI, AMPHI		
3. ANN, ENN		
4. ANTE, ANTI		
5. ANTHROP		
6. ANTI		
7. AUTO		
8. BENE		
9. BI		
10. BIO		
11. CEDE, CEED		
12. CHRON		
13. CIRCUM		
14. COM, CON, COL, COR		
15. CRED		
16. CUR		
17. DEM		
18. DICT		
19. DIS, DI, DIF		
20. EQU		
21. EU		
22. EX, ES, E		

✎ **EXERCISE 6**   Are you adding some words to your WORD LIST at the end of this book? Read over your list occasionally, and try to use a few of the words in your daily conversation.

FID—faith

Did you ever wonder how Fido got his name? He's called Fido because he's *faithful* to his master. The root FID always has something to do with *faith*. **Fidelity** means *faith*fulness, and **infidelity** means un*faith*fulness. If you are **confident**, you have *faith* in yourself, but if you are **diffident** [DI not + FID faith], you don't have *faith* in yourself; you are shy.

Sometimes, as in **confide** and several other of the following words, CON is used merely as an intensive, giving more emphasis to the root that follows.

bona fide (bo´ nuh fid) [BON good + FID faith]—*lit.* in good faith; genuine. *They made a bona fide offer on the house. The museum has a bona fide painting by Gauguin.*

confidant (kahn´ fuh dant) [CON (intensive) + FID faith]—*lit.* a person one has faith in; a person one confides in. *Her dad had been her confidant for years.*

confide (kun fid´) [CON (intensive) + FID faith]—to show faith by sharing secrets. *I'd never confide in such a gossip.*

confident (kahn´ fud unt) [CON (intensive) + FID faith]—having faith in oneself, self-assured. *My brother was confident as he walked onto the stage.*

confidential (kahn fuh den´ chul) [CON (intensive) + FID faith]—marked by intimacy or willingness to confide. *What I am going to tell you is confidential.*

diffident (dif´ uh dunt) [DIF not + FID faith]—not having faith in oneself; shy. *The youngster was diffident about speaking in public.*

fidelity (fi del´ uh tē)—faithfulness. *His fidelity to the party platform was questionable.*

infidel (in´ fuh dul) [IN not + FID faith]—*lit.* not faithful; a person who does not believe in a particular religion. *The Muslims were in conflict with the infidels.*

infidelity (in fuh del´ uh tē) [IN not + FID faith]—unfaithfulness, especially in marriage. *No one had ever accused him of infidelity.*

perfidious (per fid´ ē us) [PER through + FID faith]—deceiving through a pretense of faith; treacherous. *Her perfidious actions branded her as someone not to be trusted.*

ALSO: affidavit, confidence, perfidy

✎ EXERCISE 1   Write the appropriate FID word.

1. He owned a _____ Model T Ford.

2. Even a _____ person will enjoy the interaction of choral reading.

3. His _____ attempts to undermine the work of his own committee were shocking.

4. Anyone not following the state religion was called an _____.

5. You can be sure of his _____; he would never be unfaithful.

6. She needed a _____ with whom she could discuss her problems.

7. Juanita and her best friend _____ in each other.

8. Most employee records are _____ because they contain personal information.

9. His constant _____ caused their marriage to end.

10. Having earned "A"s and "B"s on all her tests, Kailee was _____ she would pass the final.

✎ **EXERCISE 2 REVIEW**   These paragraphs contain eight words you've studied. **Can you find all eight? Underline them. Then copy to your** *word list* **any words whose meaning you are doubtful about. Look up each of the doubtful words in the Word Index to find the page on which the word is explained. When you are sure of the meaning of all the words, read the paragraphs again.**

When I first came into this class, I was incredulous at the amount of work assigned. I almost lost my equanimity when I heard that we had to keep a daily vocabulary journal. Soon, though, I realized that the consensus of the class was that the professor is our benefactor.

For a while I was ambivalent, but finally my attitude changed until now it is the antithesis of what it was at first. I now concur with the opinion of the other students and find that I am adding an incredible number of words to my vocabulary.

✎ **EXERCISE 3 REVIEW**   Write a sentence of your own for each word. You may **use a sentence from a preceding page if you can remember it without looking back.**

1. asymmetrical

2. ambivalent

3. automaton

4. anachronism

5. anticlimax

✎ **EXERCISE 4**   Are you adding some words to your WORD LIST at the end of **this book? Read over your list occasionally, and try to use a few of the words in your daily conversation.**

GEN—birth, race, kind

In ancient mythology, when a child was born, a guardian spirit or **genius** (so named because it appeared at *birth*) was appointed to guide the person throughout life. Today, although we no longer believe we are given a guiding genius at birth, we may still have within us from *birth* a genius for something such as math or painting. Thus, the ancient guiding genius has now become an exceptional intellectual or creative ability.

    GEN has four main meanings.

1. First of all, **GEN** means *birth*—not only the *birth* of people but also the *birth* of things (an engine **generates** or gives *birth* to electricity) and the *birth* of ideas (angry words **engender** or give *birth* to hate, whereas kind words engender love).

    engender (in jen´ dur)—*lit.* to give birth to; to develop; to bring forth, as ideas or feelings. *His handling of the problem engendered the respect of his fellow workers.*

    generate (jen´ uh rāt)—*lit.* to give birth to; to produce, as an engine generates power. *By turning a windmill, the wind can generate electricity.*

    generation (jen uh rā´ shun)—all the people born at about the same time. *They were trying to understand the younger generation.*

    genesis (jen´ uh sis)—the birth or coming into being of anything; origin; creation. *His many childhood pets were the genesis of his interest in zoology.*

    genius (jen´ yus)—in ancient mythology, a guardian spirit appointed at birth to guide a person; now, an exceptional intellectual or creative ability. *She's a genius at painting.*

    hydrogen (hi´ druh jun) [HYDR water + GEN birth]—a gas so called because it generates (gives birth to) water by its combustion. *Hydrogen gas was used in the first balloons to carry men into the sky.*

    ingenious (in jen´ yus) [IN in + GEN birth]—*lit.* having inborn talent; clever at contriving. *It took an ingenious architect to design a house for such a small lot.*

    ingenuous (in jen´ yO us) [IN in + GEN birth]—*lit.* freeborn, honest; showing innocent or childlike simplicity or gullibility. *She was completely ingenuous, never questioning anything she was told.*

2. **GEN** also indicates noble or good *birth* or breeding.

    generous (jen´ uh rus)—liberal in giving as a person of noble birth would be. *In being generous is where we find our highest aspirations, our deepest good.*

    genial (je´ ne ul)—having a friendly and kindly manner. *His genial personality made him a favorite party guest.*

    genteel (jen tēl´)—having an aristocratic quality; refined in manner. *She was genteel and, therefore, unused to coarse manners.*

    gentility (jen til´ uh tē)—the condition of being genteel. *Her gentility had kept her aloof from the rest of her fellow workers.*

    gentleman (jen´ tl man)—a man of noble or gentle birth; a polite, considerate man. *If a man is just, merciful, and kindly, he is a gentleman.*

    gentry (jen´ trē)—people of gentle birth or high social position. *The town's gentry were its most powerful members.*

3. **GEN** also means *race*. If you are interested in your family history, you are interested in **genealogy,** the study of the ancestors of a family.

gene (jen)—an element of the germ plasm that transmits characteristics of the parents, and hence of the race, to a child. *Information stored in the genes determines an individual's eventual height.*
genealogy (je nē al′ uh je) [GEN race + -LOGY study of]—*lit.* the study of race; the study of family descent. *After seeing* Roots, *many people became interested in genealogy.*
genetics (juh net′ iks)—the science of heredity. *Fruit flies are often used in experiments in genetics because they reproduce so quickly.*
genocide (jen′ uh sīd) [GEN race + CID to kill]—the systematic, planned killing of a racial, political, or cultural group. *Genocide is unthinkable in any civilized society.*
progenitor (pro jen′ uh tur) [PRO forth + GEN birth]—a direct ancestor. *Their zeal for social reform could be traced to their progenitor.*
progeny (proj′ uh nē) [PRO forth + GEN birth]—children or descendants. *His progeny inherited his ambition.*

4. **GEN** also means a category or *kind*.

generic (juh ner′ ik)—general kind; commonly available; not protected by a trademark, as generic drugs. *She usually economizes by buying generic cereals instead of name brands.*
genre (zhahn′ ruh)—a particular kind or category of literature or art. *He hadn't limited his reading to a single genre but had delved into poetry, the short story, and the novel.*

ALSO: congenital, cryptogenic, degenerate, eugenics, general, heterogeneous, homogeneous, homogenize, pathogenic, primogeniture

EXERCISE 1　Write the appropriate GEN word.

1. She _____ ideas for her essays easily.
2. Her _____ behavior made her welcome wherever she went.
3. Our _____ determine most of our physical features.
4. Many prescription plans require patients to use _____ medications if available.
5. Her favorite literary _____ is the novel.
6. The _____ of most ideas begins with much thought.
7. _____ always treat ladies with respect.
8. The manager's rude behavior did not _____ respect from her workers.
9. On Father's Day, George's _____ filled his house.
10. His _____ design won his company the contract.
11. She traced her _____ to six countries on three different continents.
12. The 1994 _____ in Rwanda killed almost a million Tutsis.

EXERCISE 2   Circle the GEN word that is used correctly in each sentence.

1. The Stein family, whose (progenitors, genetics) emigrated from Germany early in the nine-teenth century, settled in New York City.
2. His father's dominant (genealogy, genes) were passed on to all his children.
3. The (genial, ingenuous) doctor had a great bedside manner, especially when it came to his older patients.
4. (Hydrogen, Gentility) is used in vegetable oils to make margarines and spreads.
5. Her (genius, generous) nature prevented her from refusing any beggar who approached her.
6. Former newscaster and Author Tom Brokaw named the people who lived through the Great Depression and World War II the "Greatest (Generation, Genre)" for all they sacrificed for their country.

EXERCISE 3   Write a sentence of your own for each GEN word.

1. engender

   _____

2. genteel

   _____

3. genocide

   _____

4. progeny

   _____

5. generic

   _____

6. genteel

   _____

EXERCISE 4 JOURNAL   Using the GEN words you just studied, write several sentences about your family in your *vocabulary journal.*

EXERCISE 5 REVIEW Write C in front of each sentence in which all the words are used correctly.

1. _____ These shoes are so ill-fitting that they will expatiate my feet and create blisters.

2. _____ State courts have general jurisdiction, meaning that they can hear any case except those prohibited by law.

3. _____ The inspector's cursory examination of the burnt house indicated the possibility of arson; a more extensive examination should be undertaken.

4. _____ The governor ordered the legislature to commensurate in special session by January 15.

5. _____ Plastic diapers pollute the earth because they are not biodegradable.

6. _____ Although the island is a colony, in most matters, it is autonomic, free from its mother country's orders.

7. _____ I look forward to our superannuated visits to the city.

8. _____ The hunters were alarmed by the atypical behavior of the wild bear.

9. _____ The movie star was far from diffident as he met with his fans.

10. _____ When Caesar realized that Brutus had betrayed him, he criticized his perfidious friend.

11. _____ Jon has been euphony ever since Jackie said yes to his marriage proposal.

12. _____ When pressed for a firm answer, she equivocated.

13. _____ American social critic and humorist H. L. Mencken defined a demagogue as "one who preaches doctrines he knows to be untrue to men he knows to be idiots."

14. _____ Colonial opposition to unfair taxation by the British was a precursor of the Revolution.

15. _____ American statesman Henry Kissinger said, "America's credibility must not be squandered, especially by its leaders."

EXERCISE 6 Are you adding words to your WORD LIST at the end of this book? Read over your list occasionally, and try to use a few of the words in your daily conversation.

GRAPH, GRAM—to write

We don't usually think of **geography** as having anything to do with writing, but it is made up of GEO, *earth,* and GRAPH, to *write,* and is actually a *writing* about the surface of the Earth. Note how each of the following words has something to do with *writing.*

autograph (aw´ tuh graf) [AUTO self + GRAPH to write]—*lit.* the writing of oneself; one's signature. *The author autographed his book for me.*

calligraphy (kuh lig´ ruh fē) [CALLI beautiful + GRAPH to write]—the art of fine handwriting. *She copied a favorite poem in beautiful calligraphy and had it framed.*

cardiogram (kahr´ de uh gram) [CARD heart + GRAM to write]—a written tracing showing the contractions of the heart. *The cardiogram showed a few extra heartbeats.*

choreography (kor e og´ ruh fē) [CHOR dance + GRAPH to write]—*lit.* the writing of a story in dance; the creating and arranging of dance movements, especially ballet. *The director of the opera also did the choreography.*

diagram (di´ uh gram) [DIA through + GRAM to write]—*lit.* a writing to show through something, to make it plain; a drawing that explains something. *We were given a diagram of the route we were to take.*

epigram (ep´ uh gram) [EPI on + GRAM to write]—*lit.* a writing on a subject; any short, witty saying. *She liked to quote the epigram "Success is getting what you want; happiness is wanting what you get."*

geography (je og´ ruh fē) [GEO earth + GRAPH to write]—*lit.* a writing about the Earth; a science dealing with the Earth and its life. *Geography was my favorite subject in grade school.*

graffiti (gra fe´ tē)—crude drawings or writings scratched on public walls. *Getting rid of graffiti on the subway walls was the next civic project.*

graphic (graf´ ik)—full of vivid details. *The author gave a graphic description of the earthquake.*

graphite (graf´ īt)—a soft, black, lustrous form of carbon found in nature and used in pencils (for writing). *Graphite has many other uses besides supplying the lead for pencils.*

hologram (ho´ luh gram) [HOLO whole + GRAM to write]—a three-dimensional photograph made using lasers. *The cover of the* National Geographic *for December 1988 was a hologram.*

monogram (mon´ uh gram) [MONO one + GRAM to write]—two or more letters entwined (written) in one design. *On each towel, she embroidered a monogram.*

monograph (mon´ uh graf) [MONO one + GRAPH to write]—a book written about one specific subject. *She published a monograph about the biblical references in Browning's poems.*

program (pro´ gram) [PRO before + GRAM to write]—*lit.* a writing beforehand; a listing of things to follow; a printed announcement of events; in computer science, a sequential set of commands to be followed by a computer. *I was the first one on the program.*

seismograph (sīz´ muh graf) [SEISMOS earthquake + GRAPH to write]—an instrument for recording (writing) the intensity and duration of an earthquake. *The seismograph recorded an earthquake that registered 7 on the Richter scale.*

stenographer (stuh nahg´ ruh fur) [STEN narrow + GRAPH to write]—*lit.* one who uses narrow or small writing (shorthand); a person who takes dictation in shorthand. *Stenographers are still used in courtroom proceedings.*

topography (tuh pahg′ ruh fē) [TOP place + GRAPH to write]—a detailed drawing (writing) on a map of the surface features of a region (place) showing their relative positions and elevations. *Before venturing into the canyon, the hikers studied its topography.*

ALSO: autobiography, bibliography, biography, cryptography, demographic, lithography, orthography, phonograph, photography, telegram, telegraph

✎ **EXERCISE 1**   **Write the appropriate GRAPH, GRAM word.**

1. His fiancée hired me to write the wedding invitations in ———————————.
2. As the audience entered the theater, the ushers handed out the ———————————.
3. She collects ——————————— of her favorite baseball players.
4. Many ——————————— appear lifelike.
5. A study of the ——————————— of the region showed many caves and hills.
6. The fence around the construction was covered with amusing ———————————.
7. Children shouldn't watch movies with ——————————— violence or themes.
8. The dancers' ——————————— made the show a success.
9. The sewing book shows three different styles of ———————————.
10. The ——————————— recorded 15 small earthquakes in a 24-hour period.
11. The court ——————————— patiently recorded every word of the ten-hour trial.
12. Knowing ——————————— helps in understanding current world events.
13. The map showed the ——————————— of the countryside.
14. One of Oscar Wilde's ——————————— frequently quoted is "I can resist everything except temptation."
15. His ——————————— showed the need for further medical tests.

✎ **EXERCISE 2 JOURNAL**   **Using the GRAPH, GRAM words you just studied, write several sentences about writing you have done your *vocabulary journal.***

✎ **EXERCISE 3**   **Continue to add words to your WORD LIST, and review the words you've already added.**

HYPER—overmuch, too far

Do you know someone who exaggerates? He or she is using **hyperbole**, a figure of speech that uses embellishment, and comes from the roots HYPER, meaning *too far* and BAINEIN, meaning *to step*. You've probably heard such expressions as "I've tried to diet a thousand times" or "Your suitcase weighs a ton!" These exaggerations, used for emphasis and not meant to be literal, are called **hyperboles**.

hyperactive (hy per ac' tiv) [HYPER overmuch + ACTUS a doing]—more active than is usual or desirable. *His hyperactive mind allowed him to think about several things at once.*

hyperbaton (hy per bah' tun) [HYPER overmuch + BAINEIN to step]—a figure of speech using inverted word order. *Yoda speaks in hyperbaton, for example, "Ready are you? What know you of ready?"*

hyperbole (hy per' bō lē) [HYPER overmuch + BAINEIN to step]—a figure of speech in which exaggeration is used for emphasis or effect. *Her hyperbole caused the audience to laugh.*

hypercritical (hy per crĭt i' cal) [HYPER overmuch + KRITIKE the art of judgment]—extremely critical. *Her hypercritical comments blocked the student's creativity.*

hyperglycemia (hy per glī cē' mē uh) [HYPER overmuch + GLYCEMIA presence of glucose in the blood]—excess sugar in the blood. *Signs of hyperglycemia are thirst, a dry mouth, and a need to urinate.*

hyperopic (hy per o' pik) [HYPER overmuch + OPTOS seen, visible]—condition of the eye in which vision is better for distant objects than for near objects; farsightedness. *After being diagnosed hyperopic, he was fitted with glasses.*

hypertension (hy per ten' shun) [HYPER overmuch + TENDERE to stretch]—abnormally high blood pressure. *People with hypertension are at risk for heart disease.*

hypertrophy (hy per' trō fē) [HYPER overmuch + TROPHY food, nourishment]—exaggerated growth. *His extensive weight-lifting led to hypertrophy of his biceps.*

✎ **EXERCISE 1**   Match the HYPER word to its definition; there is one extra definition.

1. _____ hyperactive
2. _____ hyperbaton
3. _____ hyperopic
4. _____ hyperbole
5. _____ hypertension
6. _____ hypertrophy

7. _____ hyperglycemia
8. _____ hypercritical

A. abnormally high blood pressure
B. exaggerated growth
C. more active than is usual or desirable
D. farsightedness
E. extremely critical
F. figure of speech in which exaggeration is used for emphasis or effect
G. excess sugar in the blood
H. a figure of speech using inverted word order

✎ **EXERCISE 2**   Write the correct HYPER word.

1. Because she was _____ in most aspects of her life, she had few friends.
2. Some authors use _____ to add humor to their stories.
3. My eye doctor offered information about the causes of my _____ vision.
4. Using steroids can lead to muscle _____.
5. Along with alliteration, _____ is usually found in poetry.
6. Dave's doctor was concerned about his _____, fearing it may affect his heart.
7. A common cause of chronic _____ is obesity.
8. The _____ child exhausted her mother.

✎ **EXERCISE 3 REVIEW**   Underline the vocabulary word used correctly in the sentence.

1. Albert Einstein was an (ingenious, ingenuous) mathematician.
2. My mother is my (confident, confidant) and best friend.
3. Jenna decided to take the job offer and (emigrate, enervate) to Peru.
4. Having earned straight "A"s on her report card, Kendra was in a state of (euphony, euphoria).
5. The burglar left the shop in (disarray, dissuade).
6. The dictator issued an (addict, edict) forbidding protests.
7. Islands are especially likely to develop (endemic, epidemic) species because of their geographical isolation.
8. Ridding the cabin of ants was a (concurrent, recurrent) activity.
9. The traveling salesman completed his (circuit, circumvent) every two months.
10. Physical therapists use (biosphere, biofeedback) to help stroke victims regain movement in paralyzed muscles.

✎ **EXERCISE 4 JOURNAL**   Using HYPER words you just studied, write several sentences in your *vocabulary journal.*

✎ **EXERCISE 5**   Are you adding some words to your WORD LIST at the end of this book? The best way to improve your vocabulary is to use your words.

EXERCISE 6 REVIEW   For each word, give the root and its meaning.

WORD	ROOT	MEANING
1. asymmetrical		
2. synchronize		
3. credulity		
4. demagogue		
5. misanthrope		
6. choreography		
7. engender		
8. ebullient		
9. benefit		
10. euphoria		
11. bona fide		
12. antedate		
13. antagonist		
14. disburse		
15. convivial		

LOG—speech, word

Words containing the root LOG have to do with *speech*. A **monologue** is a *speech* by one person. A **dialogue** is *speech* between two or more people. A **prologue** is a *speech* before a play, and an **epilogue** is a *speech* after it. (Note that all of these words can also be spelled without the *ue* ending.)

analogous (uh nal′ uh gus) [ANA according to + LOG speech, reason]—similar in some ways but not in others. *The wings of a bird and those of an airplane are analogous, having a similar function but a different origin and structure.*

analogy (uh nal′ uh je) [ANA according to + LOG speech, reason]—resemblance in some particulars between things otherwise unlike. *To get his point across, the professor used the following analogy: Cutting classes is like paying for a hamburger and then walking away without eating it.*

apology (a pol′ uh je) [APO away + LOG speech]—lit. a speaking away; a speech expressing regret for a fault or offense. *I offered him an apology for my rude behavior.*

dialogue (di′ uh log) [DIA between + LOG speech]—speech between two or more people; a conversational passage in a play or narrative. *After a long dialogue, we finally resolved our difficulties.*

doxology (dok sol′ uh je) [DOX praise + LOG speech]—a hymn or expression of praise to God. *The best-known doxology is the one sung in Protestant churches, beginning "Praise God from whom all blessings flow."*

epilogue (ep′ uh log) [EPI on + LOG speech]—a speech directed to the audience at the conclusion of a play. *Shakespeare's plays often end with an epilogue spoken by one of the characters.*

monologue (mon′ uh log) [MONO one + LOG speech]—a speech by one person; a soliloquy. *The monologue beginning "Is this a dagger which I see before me?" helps reveal Macbeth's character.*

prologue (pro′ log) [PRO before + LOG speech]—a speech before a play. *Romeo and Juliet begins with a prologue that summarizes the story for the audience.* Also, any introductory event. *The fancy appetizers were the prologue to an excellent dinner.*

travelogue (trav′ uh log) [TRAVEL journey + LOG speech]—a speech or film about travel. *We heard a travelogue about Greenland.*

ALSO: analog, decalogue, eulogy, logic

✎ EXERCISE 1   Match each LOG word with its definition.

1. _____ doxology
2. _____ analogy
3. _____ epilogue
4. _____ prologue
5. _____ dialogue

A. resemblance in some ways between things otherwise unlike
B. a speech before a play
C. a speech between two or more people
D. a hymn or expression of praise to God
E. a speech directed to the audience at the end of a play

✎ EXERCISE 2   **Write the appropriate LOG word.**

1. His _____ seemed sincere.

2. The _____ convinced us to go to Australia.

3. In *The Lord of the Rings*, Sam and Bilbo have a spirited _____ about the Golem.

4. Her first complaint was just a _____ of what was to come.

5. Hamlet's "To be or not to be" is the most famous _____ in English literature.

6. Reading a book is _____ to dropping chemicals into a test tube: There should be a reaction.

✎ EXERCISE 3 REVIEW   **Write C in front of each sentence in which all words are used correctly.**

1. _____ The term "laid to rest" is a euphemism for "buried."

2. _____ The hydrogen-filled balloon slipped out of the toddler's hand and rose toward the clouds.

3. _____ The graphite showed the contractions of the heart.

4. _____ The demagogue was only interested in gaining power.

5. _____ The pig was dissected by the biology students.

6. _____ Having a daily plan is equinox for students.

7. _____ The prologue was the perfect conclusion to the play.

8. _____ Geography and math are my two favorite subjects.

9. _____ The prepared student was confident he would do well on the examination.

✎ EXERCISE 4 REVIEW   **Match each word to its correct word root.**

1. _____ ANTI

2. _____ ANTHROP

3. _____ BIO

4. _____ CIRCUM

5. _____ CHRON

6. _____ CRED

7. _____ GEN

8. _____ HYPER

A. around

B. birth, race, kind

C. time

D. to believe

E. against, opposite

F. life

G. human

H. overmuch, too far

-LOGY—study of

-LOGY at the end of a word usually means *study of*. **Biology** [BIO life] is the *study of* plant and animal life. **Geology** [GEO earth] is the *study of* the history of the Earth, especially as recorded in rocks. **Etymology** [ETYM true] is the *study of* the origin (true meaning) and development of words. In this book, you are getting an introduction to etymology.

Almost all such words have O in front of the -LOGY so that the ending is -OLOGY. But two words have A in front of the -LOGY—genealogy and mineralogy.

archeology (ahr ke ol' uh je) [ARCH ancient + -LOGY study of]—the study of ancient cultures based on artifacts and other remains. *Egypt is a good place to study archeology because the monuments and artifacts are well preserved.*

anthropology (an thruh pol' uh je) [ANTHROP human + -LOGY study of]—a study of the physical, social, and cultural development and behavior of human beings. *Shanna studied anthropology's understanding of Aboriginal society and its traditional gender relations.*

astrology (uh strol' uh je) [ASTR star + -LOGY study of]—a pseudoscience claiming to foretell the future by a study of the stars. *To try to foresee her future, she consulted a book on astrology.*

ecology (e kol' uh je) [ECO home + -LOGY study of]—the study of the relationship between organisms and their environment (home). *The ecology of the region showed that the number of wild animals had decreased as a result of lumbering.*

embryology (em bre ol' uh je)—the study of the formation and development of embryos. *The science of embryology has determined the exact times when various parts of an embryo develop.*

entomology (en tuh mol' uh je) [EN in + TOM to cut + -LOGY study of]—the study of insects (whose bodies are "cut" in three segments). *The entomology class was studying grasshoppers.*

etymology (et uh mol' uh je) [ETYM true + -LOGY study of]—the study of the origin (true meaning) and development of words. *From his study of etymology, he learned many interesting word histories.*

geology (je ol' uh je) [GEO earth + -LOGY study of]—the study of the history of the Earth, especially as recorded in rocks. *The geology of the Grand Canyon shows various periods in the Earth's development.*

meteorology (me te uh rol' uh je) [METEORA things in the air + -LOGY study of]—the study of the atmosphere, especially weather and weather conditions. *The Bureau of Meteorology is recording slight changes in climate from year to year.*

ornithology (awr nuh thol' uh je) [ORNITH bird + -LOGY study of]—the branch of zoology dealing with birds. *Because he was interested in ornithology, he made recordings of bird songs.*

psychology (si kol' uh je) [PSYCH mind + -LOGY study of]—the study of mental processes and behavior. *His study of psychology helped him understand himself.*

ALSO: bacteriology, biology, chronology, dermatology, genealogy, gynecology, mineralogy, morphology, paleontology, pathology, physiology, technology, theology, zoology

✎ **EXERCISE 1**   What science makes a study of the following? Write the appropriate -LOGY word.

1. the human mind _____
2. weather conditions _____
3. the origin and development of words _____
4. the history of the Earth as recorded in rocks _____
5. ancient cultures based on their artifacts and monuments _____
6. insects _____
7. birds _____
8. embryos _____
9. the relationship of organisms to their environment _____

✎ **EXERCISE 2**   Fill in the correct -LOGY word.

1. Forensic _____ applies insect evidence to criminal investigations.
2. People who study _____ believe that it has an influence on the course of the natural world.
3. _____ is the subdivision of developmental biology that studies embryos and their development.
4. Because _____ is study of the physical, social, and cultural development and behavior of human beings, it answers the question "What are we?"
5. When you study vocabulary, you are studying _____.

✎ **EXERCISE 3 REVIEW**   In this book, you have been studying etymology. List five words—and the etymology of each—that you have found most interesting.

LOQU, LOC—to speak

A **soliloquy** [SOL alone + LOQU to speak] is a *speech* given by an actor, alone on the stage, to reveal private thoughts and emotions. The most famous soliloquy, of course, is Hamlet's "To be or not to be," when Hamlet reveals his feelings to the audience. Another soliloquy from a Shakespearean play is the opening speech of *Richard III*, "Now is the winter of our discontent. . . ."

colloquial (kuh lo´ kwe ul) [COL together + LOQU to speak]—like the language used when people speak together informally; informal or conversational. *"Passing the buck" is a colloquial expression for "shifting responsibility."*

colloquium (kuh lo´ kwe um) [COL together + LOQU to speak]—*lit.* a speaking together; an academic seminar on some field of study, led by several experts. *They attended the colloquium on Hemingway.*

eloquent (el´ uh kwunt) [E out + LOQU to speak]—*lit.* speaking out; fluent; persuasive. *The audience was moved by the eloquent speaker.*

grandiloquent (gran dil´ uh kwunt) [GRAND grand + LOQU to speak]—marked by a lofty, extravagantly colorful style. *The Duke tries to impress Huckleberry Finn with his grandiloquent speech.*

loquacious (lo kwa´ shus)—talkative. *It was my luck to get a loquacious bridge partner.*

soliloquy (suh lil´ uh kwe) [SOL alone + LOQU to speak]—a speaking alone to oneself, as in a drama; a monologue. *The soliloquy is used less frequently in modern drama than in earlier plays.*

ventriloquist (ven tril´ uh kwist) [VENTR stomach + LOQU to speak]—*lit.* one who speaks from the stomach; one who speaks so that the sounds seem to come from somewhere other than the speaker's mouth. *The ventriloquist was able to speak without moving his lips while manipulating the lower jaw of the puppet on his lap.*

ALSO: circumlocution, colloquy, elocution, eloquence, interlocutor, loquacity, obloquy

✎ EXERCISE 1   Write the appropriate LOQU, LOC word.

1. She was so _____ that no one else had a chance to say anything.

2. He uses a(n) _____ rather than a formal style of writing.

3. The lecturer hoped his _____ style of speaking, with big words and impressive gestures, would make up for his lack of ideas.

4. A dramatist may reveal a character's feelings to the audience through a(n) _____ .

5. The man with the puppet on his knee was a(n) _____ .

6. Sixty professors took part in the _____ on hazardous waste.

7. The audience responded with a standing ovation to his _____ speech.

✎ **EXERCISE 2 JOURNAL**   Using the LOQU, LOC words you just studied, write several sentences in your *vocabulary journal.*

✎ **EXERCISE 3 REVIEW**   Write C in front of each sentence in which all your vocabulary words are used correctly.

1. _____ Radio is the precursor of television.

2. _____ Jerry did a great job of maintaining his equanimity, right up until he fell into the orchestra pit.

3. _____ The suit for divorce accused him of gentility.

4. _____ The heartless old general felt no compunction about sending those men into battle because, he said, "Wasn't nobody gonna miss 'em."

5. _____ Meteorology has now made weather prediction more accurate.

6. _____ Always interested in butterflies, she decided to major in entomology.

7. _____ They were repainting the fence to get rid of the objectionable graffiti.

8. _____ The disconsolate widow spent the afternoon drinking champagne and dancing with her friends.

9. _____ Not knowing a word of French, the traveler found herself without a single confident to whom to tell her troubles.

10. _____ Through the study of genetics, scientists are making discoveries about heredity.

11. _____ They own a bona fide Seth Thomas clock dating from 1850.

12. _____ My mother's secret was using several diffident apples in her pies.

13. _____ Parents who are hypercritical may discourage their children from trying new activities.

14. _____ In order to recede, you have to give all your attention to your task.

15. _____ The two sides opened a dialogue to try to reach a compromise.

MAL—bad

In the medieval calendar, two days in each month were marked as *dies mali* (evil days)—January 1 and 25, February 4 and 26, March 1 and 28, April 10 and 20, May 3 and 25, June 10 and 16, July 13 and 22, August 1 and 30, September 3 and 21, October 3 and 22, November 5 and 28, and December 7 and 22. Any enterprise begun on one of these *bad days* was certain to end in failure. Our word **dismal** comes from *dies mali*, but today a dismal day is merely gloomy or depressing.

Was he really ill when he stayed at home from work during the week of the World Series, or was he just malingering? **Malinger** originally meant to be in *bad* health, but, as with many words, it has changed over the years and now means to pretend to be ill in order to avoid duty or work. If you stay home from work pretending to be ill, you're malingering. If you claim you have a bad back when the walks need shoveling, if you develop a headache when you're supposed to go to a boring meeting, if you are too weary after dinner to help with the dishes—you could be malingering.

A number of words beginning with MAL are easy to understand because MAL simply gives the word a "bad" meaning.

malnutrition is bad nutrition
maltreated means badly treated
maladjusted means badly adjusted to the circumstances of one's life
malfunction means to function badly, as an engine malfunctions
malpractice means improper treatment of a patient by a physician

maladroit (mal uh droit´)—not adroit; not skillful; awkward; clumsy. *The new supervisor was maladroit in dealing with the employees.*

malady (mal´ uh dē)—*lit.* a bad condition; a disease. *Science has reduced the number of incurable maladies.*

malaise (mal az´) [MAL bad + AISE ease]—a vague feeling of illness or depression. *As she was preparing for the interview, a slight malaise came over her.*

malapropism (mal′ uh prop iz uhm)—*lit.* badly appropriate; not appropriate; a ludicrous misuse of a word that sounds somewhat like the word intended. (From Sheridan's play *The Rivals* in which Mrs. Malaprop misuses words, as when she speaks of a shrewd awakening instead of a rude awakening.) *Archie Bunker made television viewers of the seventies laugh at his malapropisms, as when he said, "The donor may wish to remain unanimous."*

malaria (muh ler′ ē uh) [MAL bad + AER air]—a disease once thought to be caused by bad air from the swamps. *Malaria is often contracted in the tropics.*

malcontent (mal′ kun tent)—*lit.* one who is badly contented; a discontented or rebellious person. *He was a born malcontent, always complaining.*

malediction (mal uh dik′ shun) [MAL bad + DICT to speak]—a curse (opposite of benediction). *The leader of the cult pronounced a malediction upon all who did not follow him.*

malevolent (muh lev′ uh lunt) [MAL bad + VOL to wish]—wishing evil toward others. *The defendant cast a malevolent glance toward his accuser.*

malfeasance (mal fē zuns) [MAL bad + FAC to do]—wrongdoing, especially by a public official. *The mayor was accused of malfeasance in his distribution of public funds.*

malice (mal′ is)—active bad feeling or ill will. *The past president felt no malice toward the candidate who defeated him.*

malicious (muh lish′ us)—intentionally bad or harmful. *She refused to listen to malicious gossip.*

malign (muh lin e′)—to speak evil of; to slander. *In the political debate, his opponent maligned him.*

malignant (muh lig′ nunt)—bad or harmful; likely to cause death. *The biopsy revealed that the growth was not malignant.*

malinger (muh ling′ gur)—to pretend to be in bad health to get out of work. *Since his headaches always occurred just at schooltime, we thought he was malingering.*

ALSO: malefactor, malformed, malocclusion, malodorous

✎ EXERCISE 1   Write the appropriate MAL word.

1. The doctor announced that the patient's _____ was chronic.
2. Even though the school conditions were ideal, the _____ always found something to complain about.
3. The doctor found a _____ tumor in her patient's liver.
4. The senator _____ his opponent by claiming she was taking bribes.
5. Teenagers often spread _____ gossip about each other.
6. When I woke up this morning, I felt a general _____ even before I remembered the sad events of the weekend.
7. When the kickbacks were discovered, the commissioner was accused of _____.
8. According to the Bible, Moses laid a _____ on the Egyptians, leading to the ten plagues.
9. The insurance investigator warned the man not to _____, or he would lose his disability payments.
10. I had to take _____ pills before entering the Congo River Basin.
11. In her attempt to sound sophisticated, she often said _____ instead.
12. In earlier centuries, teachers forced all students to write right-handed; left-handed students were considered _____.
13. The enemy turned his _____ gaze on his foe.
14. The outgoing student union president felt no _____ toward his winning opponent.

✎ EXERCISE 2 REVIEW   Write C in front of each sentence in which all words are used correctly.

1. _____ I find jogging enervating and always feel exhausted afterward.
2. _____ Her perfidious dealings were shocking because she had been such a trusted employee.
3. _____ I give little credence to the testimony of such an untrustworthy witness.

4. _____ In his study of his genealogy, he discovered that his ancestors had once lived in Holland.

5. _____ Concern about what is happening to our environment has led to a new interest in ecology.

6. _____ The suit against him charged him with fidelity to the company he worked for.

7. _____ After losing her job, she was disconsolate.

8. _____ Trying to cross the little stream on a log, I lost my equilibrium.

✎ **EXERCISE 3 REVIEW**   **Using the following ten words, fill in the blanks in the paragraph so that it makes sense. After you check your answers in the back of the book, reread the paragraph and see how satisfying it is to read a paragraph in which you are sure of all the words.**

ambiguous	graphic	consensus
anticlimax	democracy	engender
grandiloquent	perennial	eulogize
malign		

Our political conventions are a _____ example of _____ at work. Before the convention, the committee platform must reach a _____ on a platform that will be _____ enough to avoid offending anyone, yet strong enough to _____ support. At the convention itself, _____ speeches _____ the candidates and _____ the opposition. Finally, although the actual choice of a candidate is often an _____ because the outcome has been known all along, the convention does answer the _____ human question, "Who shall lead?"

✏ EXERCISE 4 REVIEW   Give the meaning of each root and a word in which it is found.

ROOT	MEANING	WORD
1. A, AN	_____	_____
2. AMBI, AMPHI	_____	_____
3. ANN, ENN	_____	_____
4. ANTE, ANTI	_____	_____
5. ANTHROP	_____	_____
6. ANTI	_____	_____
7. AUTO	_____	_____
8. BENE	_____	_____
9. BI	_____	_____
10. BIO	_____	_____
11. CEDE, CEED	_____	_____
12. CHRON	_____	_____
13. CIRCUM	_____	_____
14. COM, CON, COL, COR	_____	_____
15. CRED	_____	_____
16. CUR	_____	_____

ROOT	MEANING	WORD
17. DEM	_____	_____
18. DICT	_____	_____
19. DIS, DI, DIF	_____	_____
20. EQU	_____	_____
21. EU	_____	_____
22. EX, ES, E	_____	_____
23. FID	_____	_____
24. GEN	_____	_____
25. GRAPH, GRAM	_____	_____
26. HYPER	_____	_____
27. LOG	_____	_____
28. -LOGY	_____	_____
29. LOQU, LOC	_____	_____
30. MAL	_____	_____

EXERCISE 5 REVIEW   Try to make a word chain similar to the one on pages 1–3. Start with a word like *autocracy,* and refer to the proceeding pages to find the words you need. You may have to make several starts before you get a chain of the length you want. You should do that here, and when you are satisfied, copy your chain to one of the blank pages at the end of this book.

METER, METR—measure

Although for years Americans have used the root METER in such words as **thermometer, barometer, speedometer,** and **odometer,** we are dragging our feet in adopting the **metric system.** Only two other countries in the world don't use metric: Liberia and Myanmar (formerly called Burma). But now, with many states requiring metric instruction in the schools, perhaps we will eventually go along with the rest of the metric world.

barometer (bu rahm´ uh tur) [BAR pressure + METER measure]—an instrument for measuring atmospheric pressure and hence for assisting in predicting probable weather changes. *Since the barometer reading is falling, I'm afraid we may have a storm.*

geometry (je ahm´ uh trē) [GEO earth + METR measure]—*lit.* Earth measuring; originally, the system of measuring distances on Earth through the use of angles; now, a branch of mathematics that deals with points, lines, planes, and solids. *I find geometry easier than algebra.*

kilometer (kuh lom´ uh tur) [KILO thousand + METER measure]—1,000 meters; approximately 0.62 mile. *In Canada, the speed limits are posted in kilometers.*

metric system (me´ trik)—a decimal system of weights and measures based on the meter as a unit length and the kilogram as a unit mass. *The metric system is used almost worldwide.*

metronome (met´ ruh nōm) [METR measure + NOM law]—a clocklike instrument for measuring the exact time (law) in music by a regularly repeated tick. *Practicing the piano with a metronome helped her keep perfect time.*

odometer (o dom´ uh tur) [OD road + METER measure]—*lit.* a road measure; an instrument for measuring the distance traveled by a vehicle. *His policy was to trade in his car when the odometer registered 50,000 miles.*

parameter (puh ram´ uh tar) [PARA beside + METER measure]—a fixed limit or boundary. *Stay within the parameters of the present budget.*

pedometer (pi dom´ uh tur) [PED foot + METER measure]—an instrument that measures the distance walked by recording the number of steps taken. *To make sure she walked two miles a day, she took a pedometer with her.*

perimeter (puh rim´ uh tur) [PERI around + METER measure]—the boundary around an area. *An old rail fence ran along the perimeter of his farm.*

symmetrical (si met´ ri kul) [SYM together + METR measure]—*lit.* measured together; having both sides exactly alike. *He made a symmetrical flower arrangement for the center of the table.*

tachometer (ta kahm´ uh tur) [TACH speed + METER measure]—an instrument used to measure the speed of a revolving shaft in revolutions per minute. *My tachometer indicated that my engine was going too fast.*

trigonometry (trig uh nom´ uh trē [TRI three + GON angle + METR measure]—the branch of mathematics that deals with the relations between the sides and angles of triangles and the calculations based on these. *Her knowledge of trigonometry was of value in her surveying job.*

ALSO: asymmetrical, centimeter, chronometer, diameter, isometric, micrometer, pentameter, telemetry, thermometer

✎ **EXERCISE 1**   Which METER or METR word names or describes the following?

1. the boundary around an area ———————————————
2. an instrument that measures atmospheric pressure —————————————
3. an instrument for measuring the distance traveled by a vehicle ———————————
4. approximately 0.62 mile ————————————————
5. an instrument that measures time in music by a regularly repeated tick —————————
6. an instrument that measures the distance walked by recording the number of steps taken

   ————————————————
7. having both sides exactly alike —————————————
8. an instrument used to measure the revolutions per minute of a revolving shaft

   ——————————
9. a fixed limit or boundary —————————————
10. Earth measuring; now a branch of mathematics that deals with points, lines, planes, and
    solids —————————————

✎ **EXERCISE 2 REVIEW**   Underline the appropriate word.

1. He spent a (disproportionate, diverse) amount of time on the first part of the book.
2. The students were bored as the professor (expatiated, equivocated) about his pet theory.
3. Instead of reading my report carefully, the supervisor gave it only a (dictatorial, cursory) glance.
4. I couldn't get a word in with that (loquacious, colloquial) man.
5. She felt (disconcerted, enervated) by the confusing geometry problem in her trigonometry course.
6. Gorillas, chimps, and apes are considered (anthropomorphic, anthropoids).
7. The (confident, diffident) teenager spent most of his time sitting by himself at the party.
8. After working all day in the garden, I finally (eradicated, excavated) all the poison ivy.
9. After the spring (equanimity, equinox), the sun continues to follow a high path through the sky, with the days growing longer and longer.
10. The (disparity, discomfit) between the bride's and groom's ages surprised many of their guests.

✎ **EXERCISE 3**   Add a few more words to your WORD LIST. Record words that you have heard in your classes, at work, or in conversation.

MIT, MIS, MISS—to send

The MIT, MIS, MISS root has to do with sending. A **mission** is a task that one is *sent* to do. A **missionary** is someone *sent* out to do religious work. A **message** is a communication *sent* to someone, and the person who carries the message is a **messenger**.

dismiss (dis mis´) [DIS away + MISS to send]—to send away. *The professor dismissed the class.*

emissary (em´ uh ser ē) [E out + MISS to send]—a person sent out on a specific mission. *The government sent an emissary to look into the matter.*

intermittent (in tur mit´ unt) [INTER between + MIT to send]—*lit.* sent between intervals; stopping and starting at intervals. *The intermittent rain didn't prevent them from enjoying the game.*

missile (mis´ ul) [MISS to send]—a weapon that is fired or otherwise sent toward a target. *They fired the missile toward the enemy.*

missive (mis´ iv)—a letter or message that is sent. *A missive from the president directed their next move.*

omit (ō mit´) [OB away + MIT to send]—*lit.* to send away; to leave out. *You'd better omit that unnecessary paragraph.*

permit (pur mit´) [PER through + MIT to send]—*lit.* to send through; to allow. *The tutor won't permit unnecessary talking.*

premise (prem´ is) [PRE before + MIS to send]—*lit.* a statement sent before; an initial statement that is assumed to be true and upon which an argument is based. *His argument failed because he started with a false premise.*

promise (prahm´ us) [PRO forth + MIS to send]—*lit.* to send forth; to indicate what may be expected. *I promise to help you.*

transmission (trans mish´ un) [TRANS across + MISS to send]—a device that sends (across) power from the engine of an automobile to the wheels. *The transmission in his car is giving him trouble.* Also, the act of transmitting. *Their office requested immediate transmission of the document.*

transmit (trans mit´) [TRANS across + MIT to send]—to send (across) from one place or person to another. *The lawyer will transmit the document to his client.*

ALSO: admit, commission, commit, commitment, committee, demise, emit, intermission, omission, remiss, remission, remit, submit

EXERCISE 1   Write the appropriate MIT, MIS, MISS word.

1. The district attorney refused to _____ the charges against the student who was accused of shoplifting.

2. Students often _____ vital supporting details in their essays.

3. The embassy's _____ was called upon to settle the dispute between the neighboring countries.

4. In order for an argument to be valid, it must have a logical _____ to back it.

5. The _____ noise from the jackhammer lasted all day, disrupting our studying.

EXERCISE 2 REVIEW   Write C in front of each sentence in which all words are used correctly.

1. _____ To eradicate is literally to tear out by the roots.
2. _____ Equinox refers to an Eskimo dwelling.
3. _____ Ornithology is the study of birds.
4. _____ They have diverse interests; he likes music and she likes sports.
5. _____ Equilateral describes measurements along the equator.
6. _____ The refugee claimed to be a descendent from his country.
7. _____ A loquacious person talks too little.
8. _____ A prologue comes at the beginning of a play and an epilogue at the end.
9. _____ Malaria continues to kill over 1 million African children per year.
10. _____ An equivocal answer could be interpreted two ways.
11. _____ Malaise is a vague feeling of illness or depression.
12. _____ The malingerer sat too long over meals.
13. _____ The graphic pictures on the screen were quite disturbing.
14. _____ The movie star tried to circumvent the film's release.
15. _____ Your pedometer tells you how far you have driven.
16. _____ In Shakespearean plays, one actor often speaks alone in a soliloquy.
17. _____ In the story of Aladdin, the infidels parry with the palace guards.
18. _____ Until they formed a union, the coal miners were malcontent with their working conditions.
19. _____ Damon didn't like to emit that he made mistakes.
20. _____ The study of archeology bridges cultural gaps.
21. _____ The exchange of $24 in beads for Manhattan Island was equable.
22. _____ He avoided big words for fear he'd use a malapropism.
23. _____ The demographers collected data for the census.
24. _____ A colloquium was held to discuss the diseases now found in developing nations.
25. _____ The judge had a benign attitude toward first offenders.

MONO—one

There are two roots meaning *one*—UNI (as in **unanimous, unify, unison**) and MONO. MONO is found is such words as **monoplane** (having only *one* pair of wings), **monarchy** (having *one* ruler), and **monotheism** (belief in *one* God). Two words we don't usually think of as containing MONO are monk and monastery. A **monk** was originally *one* religious man living alone, and a **monastery** was a dwelling place for monks living in seclusion from the world.

monarchy (mahn´ ahr key) [MONO one + ARCH ruler]—a government with one hereditary ruler. *At the end of the war, the monarchy became a democracy.*

monastery (mahn´ uh ster ē)—a dwelling place for monks living secluded from the world. *The monastery was high in the mountains.*

monk (munk)—originally, one religious man living alone; now, a member of a religious brotherhood living in a monastery. *The monks formed a school for the disabled.*

monocle (mon´ uh kul) [MONO one + OCUL eye]—an eyeglass for one eye. *The English gentleman looked at us through his monocle.*

monogamy (muh nog´ uh mē) [MONO one + GAM marriage]—marriage to only one person at a time. *Monogamy is practiced in most countries today.*

monolith (mon´ uh lith) [MONO one + LITH stone]—one single large piece of stone, as a monument or a statue. *The monoliths at Stonehenge were transported from a great distance in prehistoric times.*

monolithic (mon uh lith´ ik) [MONO one + LITH stone]—like one single stone, hence solid, massive, and uniform. *The corporation had become monolithic with one strong central organization.*

monopoly (muh nahp´ uh lē) [MONO one + POLY to sell]—exclusive control by one group of a commodity or service. *The student store had a monopoly on selling college sweatshirts.*

monosyllable (mon´ uh sil uh bul)—a word of one syllable. *She thought she had to speak to the child in monosyllables.*

monotheism (mon´ uh thē iz um) [MONO one + THE god]—the belief that there is only one God. *Unlike their neighbors, the early Hebrews held to monotheism.*

monotone (mon´ uh tōn) [MONO one + TON tone]—having one tone; lack of variety in tone. *Because the professor always spoke in a monotone, his students fell asleep.*

monotonous (muh not´ nus) [MONO one + TON tone]—*lit.* one tone; having no variation. *Her constant complaints became monotonous.*

ALSO: monochromatic, monogamous, monogram, monograph, monologue, mononucleosis, monoplane, monopolize, monorail, monotony

✏️ EXERCISE 1 Write the appropriate MONO word.

1. At least it's easy to tell where the accent falls in a _____.

2. _____ is the central belief of Christians, Jews, and Muslims.

3. Her speeches are boring because she speaks in a _____.

4. The island tribe practiced _____ and had strong taboos against marital infidelity.
5. The company was _____, with a reputation for uniform policy in all its branches.
6. In Tonga, we saw huge _____ that had been set up in prehistoric times.
7. During the seventeenth century, most European countries were ruled by a _____.
8. Most people wear bifocals rather than a _____.
9. During the Middle Ages, _____ hand-wrote the Bible in Latin.
10. Wearing all one color of clothes is considered _____.
11. The _____ was built out of stone in the thirteenth century.

EXERCISE 2 REVIEW   Write C in front of each sentence in which all words are used correctly.

1. _____ Many people think there should be a law permitting euthanasia.
2. _____ After I dismantled my transmission, I couldn't put it back together again.
3. _____ Her towels were embroidered with her monogram.
4. _____ The new plastic heart in his body ticked like a metronome.
5. _____ "All leaves are green" would be a false premise.
6. _____ They studied a map showing the topography of the area they were entering.
7. _____ A cardiogram is a short, witty saying.
8. _____ The governor issued an edict forbidding government workers to strike.
9. _____ Intermittent showers in Hawaii are called "liquid sunshine."
10. _____ The jury exonerated him, and he was imprisoned for life.
11. _____ She felt no malice toward the person who had been hired to replace her.
12. _____ He had recently contracted a congenital malady.
13. _____ A genial clerk took time to explain why my steam iron had malfunctioned.
14. _____ The job he was given was not commensurate with his ability.
15. _____ Her hyperglycemia is treated with medicine, exercise, and diet.

EXERCISE 3 JOURNAL   In your *vocabulary journal,* describe someone you know who is always complaining about ill health. Use some of these words: chronic, commiserate, malaise, dissuade, concur, malady.

MORPH—form

MORPH meaning *form* is an easy root to spot and will help clarify some difficult words. For example, **amorphous** [A without + MORPH form] refers to something that is without *form*, such as a speech that has not yet been organized, a poem that is still in an unformed state, a plan that has not yet taken shape, or some clay that is ready for the potter's wheel.

amorphous (uh mawr´ fus) [A without + MORPH form]—without definite form or shape. *His notes for his lecture were still in an amorphous state, without any plan or organization.*

anthropomorphism (an thruh po mawr´ fism) [ANTHROP human + MORPH form]—assigning human characteristics or behavior to inanimate objects or animals. *Most folktales, such as "The Ugly Duckling" and "The Fox and the Grapes," use anthropomorphism.*

ectomorphic (ek tuh mawr´ fik) [ECTO outside + MORPH form]—characterized by a slender physical build developed from the outside layer of the embryo. *With his ectomorphic build, he was never able to compete in football.*

endomorphic (en duh mawr´ fik) [ENDO inside + MORPH form]—characterized by prominence of the abdomen and other soft body parts developed from the inside layer of the embryo. *An endomorphic person has to struggle constantly against becoming overweight.*

mesomorphic (mez uh mawr´ fik) [MESO middle + MORPH form]—characterized by muscular or athletic build developed from the middle layer of the embryo. *The mesomorphic person tends to be successful in contact sports.*

metamorphosis (met uh mawr´ fuh sis) [META change + MORPH form]—change of form or shape. *A caterpillar undergoes a metamorphosis when it turns into a butterfly.*

Morpheus (mawr´ fē us)—in Greek mythology, the god of dreams and of the forms that dreaming sleepers see. *Morpheus was so named because of the forms he controlled in people's dreams.*

morphine (mawr´ fēn)—a drug used to bring sleep or ease pain (named after Morpheus). *The doctor prescribed morphine for the agonizing pain.*

morphology (mawr fol´ uh je) [MORPH form + -LOGY study of]—the branch of biology that makes a study of the form of animals or plants. *The professor specializes in the morphology of gophers.*

ALSO: anthropomorphic

✎ EXERCISE 1   Write the appropriate MORPH word.

1. She is the _____ type, full in the belly regardless of dieting.

2. He studied _____, especially the forms of roses.

3. _____ is used to help ease severe chronic pain in cancer patients.

4. Athletes tend to have _____ bodies.

5. Teachers with _____ lessons are hard to follow in a lecture.

6. _____ people are slender and envied by many dieters.

7. We observed the _____ of the tadpole into a frog.

8. _____, the Greek god of dreams, still visits us nightly.

✏️ **EXERCISE 2 REVIEW**   Write C in front of each sentence in which all words are used correctly. Then, in each remaining blank, write the word that should have been used.

1. _____ She tried to efface from her mind the scene that had just taken place.
2. _____ Hypertension affects one out of every four adults in the United States.
3. _____ At the close of the service, the minister pronounced the malediction.
4. _____ Interfering with a tribe's way of gathering food can be a form of genocide.
5. _____ We marveled at how the ancients had moved the monoliths at Stonehenge.
6. _____ She always tried to buy generic products because they are usually less expensive than brand-name products.
7. _____ The speaker was aware of the benevolent glances of his opponents.
8. _____ Eventually we will have to think in kilometers rather than in miles.
9. _____ Her handling of the problem was so maladroit that everyone was annoyed.
10. _____ The mother interceded on her child's behalf.

✏️ **EXERCISE 3 REVIEW**   What name would you apply to a person

1. who denies the existence of God? _____
2. who loves people and gives money to benefit them? _____
3. who studies the development and behavior of human beings? _____
4. who disagrees with the government? _____
5. who studies or collects antiquities? _____

✏️ **EXERCISE 4 REVIEW**   Match the word with its definition

1. _____ malfeasance   **A.** speaking alone to oneself as in a drama
2. _____ anthropology   **B.** deceiving through pretense of faith; treacherous
3. _____ soliloquy   **C.** wrongdoing, especially by a public official
4. _____ engender   **D.** to give birth to; to develop; to bring forth
5. _____ perfidious   **E.** the study of the physical, social, cultural development, and behavior of human beings

PAN—all

In his epic poem *Paradise Lost,* John Milton calls the capital of hell Pandemonium (PAN all + DAIMON demon), the home of *all* demons, a place of wild confusion and noise. Today **pandemonium** has come to mean any wild uproar or tumult.

panacea (pan uh se´ uh) [PAN all + AKOS remedy]—a remedy for all ills or difficulties. *People who join cults are often looking for a panacea for their troubles.*

Pan-American (pan uh mer´ uh kun)—including all of America, both North and South. *He hopes to participate in the Pan-American Games.*

panchromatic (pan krō mat´ ik) [PAN all + CHROM color]—sensitive to light of all colors. *The panchromatic film gave him excellent pictures.*

pandemonium (pan duh mo´ ne um) [PAN all + DAIMON demon]—the home of all demons in Milton's *Paradise Lost;* a wild uproar. *When the winning team returned, there was pandemonium.*

panoply (pan´ uh ple) [PAN all + HOPLON armor]—a full suit of armor; ceremonial attire; any magnificent or impressive array. *The woods in their full panoply of autumn foliage were an invitation to photographers.*

panorama (pan uh ram´ uh) [PAN all + HORAMA sight]—a view in all directions. *The panorama from the top of the Royal Gorge was awe-inspiring.*

pantheism (pan´ thē iz um) [PAN all + THE god]—the doctrine that God is all the laws and forces of nature and the universe. *He turned from the formal religions to a belief in pantheism.* Also, the ancient belief in and worship of all gods. *Pantheism was the religion of early Rome.*

pantheon (pan´ thē on) [PAN all + THE god]—a temple of all the gods. *They visited the Pantheon in Rome.* Also, the place of the idols of any group, or the idols themselves. *Eric Heiden skated his way into the pantheon of American Olympic heroes.*

pantomime (pan´ tuh mīm) [PAN all + MIM to imitate]—a theatrical performance in which the actors play all the parts with gestures and without speaking. *Marcel Marceau has turned the ancient dramatic form of pantomime into an art.*

ALSO: pandemic, panegyric

✎ EXERCISE 1   Write the appropriate PAN word.

1. If you invite 20 five-year-olds to a birthday party, you'd better be prepared for

_____ .

2. The medicine was supposed to be a _____ for all diseases.

3. His love of nature and reverence for natural laws almost amounted to

_____ .

4. It is worth climbing to the top of the cathedral to see the _____ of the city.

5. _____ by a good actor can be as expressive as dialogue.

6. The marching band was out on the football field in their full _____.

7. His goal was to make the _____ of famous tennis players.

8. They used _____ film for all their pictures of the Grand Canyon.

9. The _____ Games are played every summer in Brazil.

✎ EXERCISE 2 REVIEW   List the root for each meaning of it and give a word in which it is found.

MEANING	ROOT	WORD
1. yield, go, give away		
2. around		
3. together, with		
4. to believe		
5. to run		
6. people		
7. to speak		
8. not, away, apart		
9. equal		
10. good, well		
11. out		
12. faith		
13. birth, race, kind		
14. to write		
15. over		
16. speech, word		
17. study of		
18. to speak		
19. bad		
20. measure		
21. to send		
22. one		
23. form		
24. all		

PATH—feeling, suffering

Do you feel sympathy or empathy when the boy on stage has forgotten his speech? And do you feel apathy or antipathy toward the ideas a lecturer is presenting?

All four words—sympathy, empathy, apathy, and antipathy—describe *feelings* because they all contain the root PATH *feeling*. **Sympathy** [SYM together + PATH feeling) is literally *feeling* together with someone. **Empathy** [EM in + PATH feeling] is a stronger word, indicating that you identify with someone so closely that you *feel* "in" that person's position. **Apathy** [A without + PATH feeling] means lack of *feeling,* indifference. **Antipathy** [ANTI against + PATH feeling] means a *feeling* against someone or something, a strong dislike.

You will, of course, feel sympathy for the boy who is having stage fright, but if he happens to be your child, you will also feel empathy—identifying with him and participating in his suffering.

If the ideas a lecturer is presenting are boring, you'll feel apathy or indifference. You'll be apathetic, without feeling. But if you strongly disagree with the ideas, then you'll feel antipathy toward them and perhaps even toward the lecturer.

antipathy (an tip´ uh thē) [ANTI against + PATH feeling]—a feeling against someone or something; a strong dislike. *His antipathy toward those who disagreed with him was obvious.*

apathetic (ap uh thet´ ik) [A without + PATH feeling]—without feeling; indifferent. *When she failed to get a promotion, she became apathetic about her job and no longer did her best.*

apathy (ap´ uh thē) [A without + PATH feeling]—a lack of feeling; indifference. *Voter apathy was to blame for the poor turnout on Election Day.*

empathy (em´ puh thē) [EM in + PATH feeling]—*lit.* a feeling as if one were in the other person's place; an understanding so intimate that one participates in another's feelings. *Because he had been unemployed the year before, he now felt empathy for his unemployed friend.*

pathetic (puh thet´ ik)—arousing feelings of pity. *The dog's hunt for her missing pups was pathetic.*

pathological (path uh loj´ i kul)—caused by disease. *It was finally determined that her inability to concentrate was pathological.*

pathology (pa thol´ uh je) [PATH suffering + -LOGY study of]—*lit.* the study of suffering; the scientific study of the nature of disease, especially the structural and functional changes caused by disease. *The doctor preferred doing laboratory research in pathology to treating patients.*

pathos (pa´ thos)—a quality, especially in literature, that arouses feelings of pity. *My sister loves movies full of pathos, movies she can cry over.*

psychopathic (si ko path´ ik) [PSYCH mind + PATH suffering]—*lit.* suffering in the mind; mentally disordered. *The search for the psychopathic killer ended in his capture.*

sympathy (sim´ puh thē) [SYM together + PATH feeling]—*lit.* a feeling together with someone or something; a feeling for another person. *Everyone felt sympathy for the girl who lost the race.*

ALSO: pathogenic, telepathy

✎ **EXERCISE 1**   Write the appropriate PATH word.

1. She feels such _____ for her son in his struggle to make the team that it is almost as if she were trying to make it herself.

2. The _____ report from the lab showed the patient's prostate cancer level.

3. The defendant was diagnosed as _____ by the court psychiatrist and was deemed unfit for trial.

4. That politician has a(n) _____ for any opponents.

5. _____ cards are greatly appreciated at times of loss.

6. Shakespeare's love poems arouse _____ in all of us.

7. Since he lost his job, he has become so _____ that he refuses to look for another job.

8. Only 39 percent of the total U.S. population voted in the 2000 presidential election because of _____ toward the political system.

9. After hearing her cry for hours, we decided she was _____.

10. Her habit of lying was diagnosed as _____.

✎ **EXERCISE 2 REVIEW**   Match each word with its definition.

A. biennial **C.** anthropoid   **E.** amorphous   **G.** topography   **I.** discomfit
B. chronic   **D.** benevolent   **F.** anthropologist **H.** perimeter   **J.** malaise

1. _____ inclined to do good
2. _____ without definite form or shape
3. _____ occurring every two years
4. _____ resembling human beings
5. _____ one who studies the development and behavior of human beings
6. _____ continuing for a long time
7. _____ detailed drawing or map of a surface or region
8. _____ to undo, thwart plans of, make uneasy
9. _____ vague feeling of illness or depression
10. _____ boundary around an area

PED—foot

Two words containing PED were originally concerned with getting one's foot in an entanglement. **Impede** [IM in + PED foot] meant to get one's *foot* into an entanglement and thus hinder one's progress. Through the years, it has lost the meaning of the foot in an entanglement and now has come to mean merely to hinder the progress of. **Expedite** [EX out + PED foot] originally meant to get one's *foot* out of an entanglement and thus to speed up one's progress. Expedite too has lost the meaning of the foot in an entanglement and today means merely to speed the progress of, to help along. You might say that a poor vocabulary will impede your progress in college, whereas a large vocabulary will expedite your progress by helping you read with more understanding.

centipede (sen′ tuh pēd) [CENT hundred + PED foot]—a wormlike invertebrate popularly supposed to have a hundred feet. *In the tropics, centipedes invaded our cottage.*

expedient (ek spē de unt) [EX out + PED foot]—*lit.* foot out of an entanglement; advantageous; useful in getting a desired result. *It might be expedient to start writing your paper long before it is due.*

expedite (ek′ spuh dīt) [EX out + PED foot]—*lit.* to get the foot out of an entanglement; to speed the progress of; to help along. *To expedite your registration, fill out the forms ahead of time.*

expedition (ek spuh dish′ un) [EX out + PED foot]—*lit.* freeing the foot; a journey for a definite purpose. *The expedition to the North Pole brought back much scientific information.*

impede (im pēd′) [IM in + PED foot]—*lit.* to get the foot in an entanglement; to hinder the progress of. *An inability to read rapidly may impede one's academic progress.*

impediment (im ped′ uh munt) [IM in + PED foot]—*lit.* entanglement of the foot; anything that hinders. *The famous Greek orator Demosthenes had to overcome a speech impediment.*

pedal (ped′ ul) [PED foot]—a lever operated by the foot. *The little fellow could not reach the pedals on his bike.*

pedestrian (pu des′ tre un) [PED foot]—one who goes on foot; also, commonplace or dull, as a pedestrian style of writing. *This is a dangerous corner for pedestrians.*

pedigree (ped′ uh grē) [from the French PIED foot + DE of + GRUE crane]—*lit.* the foot of a crane, so called because the three-line diagram used to indicate descent looks like a crane's foot; a record of ancestry. *The collie's pedigree made him a valuable show dog.*

quadruped (kwahd′ rO ped) [QUADR four + PED foot]—a four-footed animal. *Most mammals are quadrupeds.*

ALSO: biped, pedestal, pedicure, pedometer

✎ EXERCISE 1   Write the appropriate PED word.

1. Reading my reference materials ahead of time will _____ my progress in writing my paper.

2. She thought it might be _____ to invite the boss to dinner.

3. Spraining his ankle early in the season is going to _____ his chances of winning the championship.

4. She couldn't imagine anyone wanting a dog without a(n) _____.

5. His unpopular voting record is a(n) _____ in his reelection campaign.

6. The mountaineers' _____ ended in triumph.

7. Often, teachers will comment that their students' writing is _____.

8. _____ cannot _____ a bicycle.

EXERCISE 2 REVIEW   Underline the appropriate word.

1. I'm tired of cold winters and am looking for an (equable, equitable) climate.

2. She had an (ingenuous, ingenious) way of avoiding her after-school chores.

3. The backers of the bill were (ebullient, disconsolate) when it passed.

4. He and his wife weren't troubled by the (diversion, disparity) in their salaries.

5. The perimeter of a property is the distance (across, around) it.

6. Her poetry was (euphonious, equivocal) and pleasant to listen to.

EXERCISE 3 REVIEW   Using the following five words, fill in the blanks in the paragraph so that it makes sense. After you check your answers in the back of the book, reread the paragraph and see how satisfying it is to read a paragraph in which you are sure of all the words.

beneficiaries	census	apathy
expedite	demographic	

The results of the 2000 _____ have given us a

_____ picture of the United States. Census forms were mailed to

each dwelling to _____ the task of counting the entire population.

Advertising was used to overcome the _____ that might have kept

people from filling out the forms. The facts gathered were especially important to cities and

states with population increases, for they are now the _____ of

increased funding from government programs.

EXERCISE 4 JOURNAL   In your *vocabulary journal,* list two things that have impeded your progress in mastering the words in this book and two things that have expedited your progress.

PHIL—to love

A word containing PHIL will have something to do with *love*. **Philosophy** [PHIL to love + SOPH wise] is the *love* of wisdom. A **bibliophile** [BIBL book + PHIL to love] is one who *loves* books. And a **philanthropist** [PHIL to love + ANTHROP human] is one who *loves* human beings, particularly one who gives money to benefit humanity (see page 20).

Anglophile (ang´ gluh fil) [ANGL English + PHIL to love]—one who greatly admires England, its customs, and its people. *A confirmed Anglophile, she spends every summer in England.*

bibliophile (bib´ le uh fil) [BIBL book + PHIL to love]—one who loves books; a book collector. *We discovered a small bookstore owned by a true bibliophile.*

philatelist (fi lat´ uh list) [PHIL to love + ATELEIA tax exemption (the stamp showed that the postage had been prepaid, and the receiver was exempt from further charge)]—one who loves stamps; a stamp collector. *As a philatelist, she was interested in collecting foreign stamps.*

philharmonic (fil hahr mon´ ik) [PHIL to love + HARMONIA harmony]—*lit.* loving harmony; devoted to music; a symphony orchestra. *That winter we heard the New York Philharmonic Orchestra.*

philodendron (fil uh den´ drun) [PHIL to love + DENDR tree]—*lit.* loving trees; a tropical climbing plant that likes the shade of trees. *She cultivated the philodendron plant for its showy, heart-shaped leaves.*

philosopher (fi los´ uh fur) [PHIL to love + SOPH wise]—one who loves and pursues wisdom through reasoning. *Immanuel Kant was one of the great philosophers of the eighteenth century.*

philosophy (fi los´ uh fē) [PHIL to love + SOPH wise]—the love and pursuit of wisdom through reasoning. *Socrates valued philosophy more than anything else.*

ALSO: Philadelphia, philanthropist, philanthropy, Philip, philippic, philology

✎ EXERCISE 1   Match each PHIL word with its definition.

A. philharmonic   **C.** philatelist   **E.** Anglophile

B. bibliophile   **D.** philosopher   **F.** philanthropist

1. _____ one who loves books
2. _____ one who admires England
3. _____ one who loves human beings and gives money to benefit humanity
4. _____ a stamp collector
5. _____ one who loves and pursues wisdom through reasoning
6. _____ loving harmony, devoted to music, a symphony orchestra

✎ EXERCISE 2 REVIEW   Underline the appropriate word.

1. The study of the forms of animals and plants is called (morphology, pathology).
2. Through her study of (entomology, etymology), she has learned the derivation of many words and thus improved her vocabulary.
3. The company was (monolithic, amorphous), with a strong central office controlling many branches.
4. He took a course in (calligraphy, topography) to improve his penmanship.
5. The cashier was accused of (malapropism, malfeasance) when the deficit was discovered.
6. She felt (perfidy, antipathy) toward the course, hating every moment of it.
7. The actor used (pantomime, pantheism) rather than words to present the character.
8. An interest in word roots will (impede, expedite) your learning new words.
9. The supervisor found the employee guilty of one lie after another and branded him (maladroit, perfidious).
10. Saying that entering a new college is like jumping into an icy lake is an (analogy, anecdote).
11. The (philanthropist, philatelist) showed us his collection of stamps.
12. His name was added to the (panoply, pantheon) of famous runners.
13. The census has brought about a more (equable, equitable) distribution of government funds.
14. He took the picture with (panchromatic, philharmonic) film.
15. His poor study skills (impede, expedite) his progress in learning new words.

✎ EXERCISE 3 REVIEW   As a review of some of the roots you have learned, try to make a root chain similar to the one on pages 1–3. Start with a word like *astronomy*, and refer to the preceding pages to find the words you need. You may have to make several starts before you get a chain of the length you want. When you are satisfied, copy your chain to one of the blank pages at the end of this book.

PHOB—fear

Do you refuse to stand on the observation platform of a tall building? If so, perhaps you have **acrophobia**, an excessive *fear* of high places. Do you avoid elevators? If so, you may be suffering from **claustrophobia**, an excessive *fear* of closed places.

acrophobia (ak ruh fo´ be uh) [ACRO high + PHOB fear]—an excessive or illogical fear of high places. *Because of her acrophobia, she refused to approach the rim of the canyon.*

claustrophobia (klos truh fo´ be uh) [CLAUS to close + PHOB fear]—an excessive or illogical fear of enclosed places. *His claustrophobia made him prefer an office that opened onto a balcony.*

hydrophobia (hi druh fo´ be uh) [HYDR water + PHOB fear]—an abnormal fear of water. Also, rabies (rabies was first called hydrophobia because victims were unable to swallow water). *There was an outbreak of hydrophobia among the dogs of the area.*

phobia (fo´ be uh)—an excessive or illogical fear of some particular thing or situation. *Her fear of dogs has really become a phobia.*

phobic (fo´ bik)—excessively fearful. *She had a phobic desire to avoid large crowds.*

photophobia (fo tuh fo´ be uh) [PHOT light + PHOB fear]—an abnormal intolerance of light. *Because of photophobia, he had to wear tinted glasses.*

technophobia (tek nuh fo´ be uh) [TECHN skill + PHOB fear]—*lit.* a fear of technology; computer anxiety. *She finally overcame her technophobia and completed a course called "Introduction to BASIC."*

xenophobia (zen uh fo´ be uh) [XENO foreigner + PHOB fear]—fear or hatred of foreigners or strangers. *Extreme patriotism may turn into xenophobia.*

EXERCISE 1   Write the appropriate PHOB word.

1. His eye problems were diagnosed as _____.

2. Because of his _____, he had a dread of falling that made him constantly uneasy.

3. Their lack of understanding of foreigners amounted to _____.

4. She claimed she got _____ working in a small room with no windows.

5. Wild rabbits can sometimes be the carriers of _____.

6. Many elderly people are anxious about computers and the Internet; they have

   _____.

7. Her fear of many different things amounts to a general _____.

✎ EXERCISE 2 REVIEW   Give the meaning of each root and a word in which it is found.

ROOT	MEANING	WORD
1. A, AN	_____	_____
2. ANTHROP	_____	_____
3. ANTE, ANTI	_____	_____
4. AUTO	_____	_____
5. BENE	_____	_____
6. CEDE	_____	_____
7. COM, CON, COL, COR	_____	_____
8. CUR	_____	_____
9. DICT	_____	_____
10. DIS, DI, DIF	_____	_____
11. EQU	_____	_____
12. EU	_____	_____
13. EX, ES, E	_____	_____
14. FID	_____	_____
15. GEN	_____	_____
16. GRAPH, GRAM	_____	_____
17. HYPER	_____	_____
18. LOG	_____	_____
19. -LOGY	_____	_____
20. LOQU, LOC	_____	_____
21. MAL	_____	_____
22. METER, METR	_____	_____
23. MIT, MIS, MISS	_____	_____
24. MONO	_____	_____
25. MORPH	_____	_____
26. PAN	_____	_____
27. PATH	_____	_____
28. PED	_____	_____
29. PHIL	_____	_____
30. PHOB	_____	_____

PHON—sound

Any word containing PHON always has something to do with *sound*. A **symphony** [SYM together + PHON sound] is literally *sounds* together, presumably pleasant sounds. If a *sound* is harsh or unpleasant, it is called **cacophony** [CACO bad + PHON sound], whereas smooth and harmonious *sounds*, especially words or phrases that please the ear, are called **euphony** [EU good + PHON sound] (see page 56).

cacophony (ka kof′ uh ne) [CACO bad + PHON sound]—*lit.* bad sounds; disagreeable or discordant sounds. *Only a mother can enjoy the cacophony of her child's violin practice.*

megaphone (meg′ uh fōn) [MEGA large + PHON sound]—*lit.* large sound; a cone-shaped device for making the sound of the voice greater. *The cheerleaders all had megaphones.*

microphone (mi′ kruh fōn) [MICRO small + PHON sound]—an instrument for intensifying weak (small) sounds. *The lecturer could not be heard clearly because he did not speak into the microphone.*

phonetics (fuh net′ iks)—the branch of language study dealing with speech sounds and their symbols. *A knowledge of phonetic symbols is an aid in learning to speak a new language.*

phonics (fon′ iks)—the use of the sounds of letters and groups of letters in teaching beginners to read. *The teacher used the phonics method to teach the children to read.*

phonograph (fo′ nuh graf) [PHON sound + GRAPH to write]—a machine for playing recorded (written on a disk) sounds. *My grandmother has an antique phonograph.*

polyphonic (pol ē fon′ ik) [POLY many + PHON sound]—having two or more independent melodies all harmonizing. *A polyphonic composition combines two or more melodies.*

saxophone (sak′ suh fōn) [SAX (after Adolphe Sax, the inventor) + PHON sound]—a wind instrument. *My brother now plays a saxophone.*

stereophonic (ster ē ō fon′ ik) [STEREO solid + PHON sound]—*lit.* solid sound; giving a multidimensional effect to sound. *A stereophonic record sounds like live music because it contains two separate sound tracks.*

symphony (sim′ fuh nē) [SYM together + PHON sound]—*lit.* sounds together; an orchestra; music written for an orchestra. *Our local symphony orchestra will give a concert in May.*

ALSO: antiphonal, euphonious, euphony, telephone

✎ **EXERCISE 1**   **Match the word with its definition.**

1. _____ cacophony
2. _____ phonetics
3. _____ symphony
4. _____ phonics
5. _____ euphony

A. pleasing sounds
B. an orchestra playing together
C. the use of the sounds of letters and groups of letters in teaching beginners to read
D. bad sounds, disagreeable
E. the branch of language study dealing with speech sounds and their symbols

✎ **EXERCISE 2**   Write the appropriate PHON word.

1. It was good to get out of the _____ of the office with its ringing phone and chattering people.
2. The several melodies are combined into an unusual _____ composition.
3. The _____ was named after its inventor, Adolphe Sax.
4. Even if I used a _____, I doubt anyone would hear what I'm trying to say in all this din.
5. His knowledge of _____ helped him pronounce French words correctly.

✎ **EXERCISE 3 REVIEW**   Write C in front of each sentence in which all words are used correctly. Then, in the remaining blanks, write the word that should have been used.

1. _____ It is not only philatelists who like the new commemorative stamps.
2. _____ Only a bibliophile would be interested in that tattered old book.
3. _____ I bought a bona fide 1903 Singer sewing machine at the auction.
4. _____ The two countries agreed that each would quit dropping missives on the other country.
5. _____ Her college course in ornithology led to her lifelong hobby of bird-watching.
6. _____ Her inability to sit still for even a few moments was diagnosed as pathological.
7. _____ I won't let anything impede my progress in learning new words.
8. _____ We expurgated the offensive language from the manuscript.
9. _____ Anyone with acrophobia will not want to go into the cave.
10. _____ The secretary felt circumscribed by all the regulations she had to follow.
11. _____ An emissary brought greetings from his country.

✎ **EXERCISE 4 JOURNAL**   In your *vocabulary journal,* list the best examples of cacophony, euphony, and symphony that you can think of.

POST—after

Preposterous is made up of PRE *before* and POST *after* and originally meant having the before part where the after part should be, as a horse with its head where its tail should be. Such a *before-after* animal would be preposterous or absurd. And so today, anything contrary to nature, reason, or common sense is called preposterous.

postdate (pōs dāt´) [POST after + DATE date]—to date a check or other document with a future date rather than the actual date. *Because I had no money in the bank, I postdated my check.*

posterior (pō stir´ e ur)—located behind (as opposed to anterior, located in front). *The posterior legs of the jackrabbit are stronger than the anterior ones.*

posterity (po ster´ uh tē)—those who come after; future generations. *Posterity will determine the value of his writing.*

postgraduate (post graj´ uh wut)—relating to a course of study after college graduation. *I look forward to taking a couple of postgraduate courses after I complete my undergraduate degree.*

posthumously (pos´ choo mus li)—after the death of the father, as a child born posthumously; after the death of the author, as a book published posthumously; after one's death, as an award received posthumously. *The medal of honor was awarded to him posthumously.*

Postimpressionist (post im presh´ uh nist)—*lit.* after the Impressionists; a school of painting in France in the late nineteenth century that followed the Impressionists. *Cézanne and Matisse were Postimpressionists.*

postlude (post´ lOd) [POST after + LUD to play]—a piece of music played after a church service. *The organist played a Bach fugue as a postlude.*

post meridiem (post muh rid´ ē um) [POST after + MERIDI noon]—(abbreviated P.M.) after noon. *The committee will meet at 3 P.M.*

postmortem (post mor´ tum) [POST after + MORT death]—an examination after death; an autopsy. *The postmortem revealed the cause of his death.*

postpone (pos pōn´) [POST after + PON to put]—to put off until afterward. *I usually postpone studying until the last minute.*

postscript (pō´ skript) [POST after + SCRIPT to write]—a note written after the main body of a letter (abbreviated P.S.). *Often the most interesting part of her letter was the postscript.*

preposterous (pri pos´ tur us) [PRE before + POST after]—*lit.* having the before part where the after part should be; contrary to nature, reason, or common sense; absurd. *The idea of flying to the moon was once considered preposterous.*

ALSO: postnatal, postnuptial, postoperative

✎ EXERCISE 1 JOURNAL   In your *vocabulary journal*, write about a trip you enjoyed, using at least two words that are new to your vocabulary.

✎ **EXERCISE 2**   Write the appropriate POST word.

1. Now that the poet is dead, some of his poems are being published ＿＿＿＿＿.
2. They prepared a time capsule for ＿＿＿＿＿.
3. Traveling faster than sound was once considered ＿＿＿＿＿.
4. The ＿＿＿＿＿ of a giraffe's body is less developed than the anterior.
5. During the organ ＿＿＿＿＿, the congregation left the church.
6. An entire gallery in the art museum was devoted to the works of the ＿＿＿＿＿.
7. Because the death was unexpected, a ＿＿＿＿＿ was required.
8. Banks often do not notice whether or not a check has been ＿＿＿＿＿.
9. Most undergraduate students are encouraged to take ＿＿＿＿＿ courses to earn a more advanced degree.
10. Ante meridiem is usually when I wake, and ＿＿＿＿＿ is when I go to sleep.
11. Because of an emergency at work, she had to ＿＿＿＿＿ her vacation.
12. The hastily written ＿＿＿＿＿ showed it was an afterthought.

✎ **EXERCISE 3 REVIEW**   Underline the appropriate word.

1. With no thought of (emolument, equity), the teacher spent hours helping the immigrants.
2. He would (eulogize, excoriate) his wife for the slightest error in her cooking.
3. They talked about subjects as (disparate, equivalent) as mud pies and ballet.
4. The applicant tended to (equivocate, expurgate) when his former job was mentioned.
5. I was (dismantled, disconcerted) when they excluded me from their plans.
6. A distrust of foreigners is called (technophobia, xenophobia).
7. The government was constantly threatened by the (dissidents, automatons).
8. A devoted Anglophile, he even uses a (monocle, trident) instead of glasses.
9. The manager of the hotel tried to create an (ambivalence, ambience) of luxury.
10. The society planned (biannual, biennial) meetings so the members could see each other at least twice a year.
11. The organist played a (prologue, postlude) at the end of the service.
12. He checked his distance traveled on the (barometer, odometer).
13. The surgeon was doing research in (pathology, phonetics).
14. The (hyperactive, hypercritical) boy could not stop moving even after his teacher removed him from the group.
15. (Proceed, Recede) to the front of the line.

PRE—before

PRE at the beginning of a word always means *before* and is easy to understand in such words as **preschool, premature, prehistoric, premeditate, prejudge,** and **precaution**. But sometimes, the meaning is not so obvious. For example, **precocious** [PRE before + COQUERE to cook, to ripen] originally applied to fruit that ripened early (before time). Today, it describes someone who has matured earlier than usual, particularly mentally. Children who are unusually smart for their years are called precocious. They have ripened early!

preamble (pre' am bul) [PRE before + AMBUL to walk]—*lit.* a walking before; a preliminary statement to a document. *Have you read the Preamble to the Constitution?*

precedent (pres' uh dunt) [PRE before + CED to go]—an act that goes before and may serve as an example for later acts. *By giving his prize to charity, he set a precedent that later winners followed.*

precipitate (pri sip' uh tāt) [PRE before + CAPIT head]—*lit.* to dash head-first; to hasten the occurrence of. *The scandal precipitated his ruin.*

precise (pri sis') [PRE before + CIS to cut]—*lit.* to cut off unnecessary parts beforehand; sharply defined and exact. *Her descriptions were always precise.*

preclude (pri klOd') [PRE before + CLUD to shut]—*lit.* to shut out beforehand; to make impossible by a previous action; to prevent. *His poor record with that company may preclude his getting another job.*

precocious (pri ko' shus) [PRE before + COQUERE to cook, ripen]—*lit.* ripened before time; prematurely developed, as a precocious child. *The child was precocious, having learned to read at four.*

predilection (pred l ek' shun) [PRE before + DILIGERE to love]—*lit.* to love before others; a preference. *Her predilection for classical music kept her from being an impartial judge in the music contest.*

preeminent (pre em' uh nunt) [PRE before + EMINERE to stand out]—standing out before all others. *Edison was preeminent among the inventors of his day.*

prejudice (prej' ud us) [PRE before + JUD judge]—a judgment formed beforehand without examination of the facts. *She finally realized that her intolerance of the newcomers was simply unfounded prejudice.*

prelude (prel' Od) [PRE before + LUD to play]—an introductory piece of music; a concert piece for piano or orchestra. *She played a Chopin prelude at the recital.* Also, an introductory performance or action preceding a more important one. *The passage of that law was the prelude to further civil rights legislation.*

preponderant (pri pon' dur unt) [PRE before + PONDER weight]—outweighing; having more power or importance. *The preponderant theme of the speakers was the future welfare of the institution.*

prerequisite (pre rek' wuh zit)—something required beforehand. *Algebra is a prerequisite for geometry.*

presage (pres' ij) [PRE before + SAGIRE to perceive]—to perceive beforehand; to predict. *Lack of cooperation among the employees presages trouble in the industry. Those dark clouds presage a storm.*

prevail (pri val′) [PRE before + VAL to be strong]—to be strong before all others; to win, as to prevail over the other contestants. *After years of practice, he finally prevailed over his challengers.*

prevent (pri vent′) [PRE before + VEN to come]—*lit.* to come before in order to keep from happening; to hinder. *Good farming techniques can prevent erosion.*

unprecedented (un pres′ uh den tid) [UN not + PRE before + CED to go]—never having happened before. *The sales manager took an unprecedented step when he gave the job to a teenager.*

ALSO: precede, precursor, predestination, predict, predominant, preempt, premise, preposterous, prerogative, prescribe, presentiment, preside, president, pretentious, previous

✎ EXERCISE 1 **Write the appropriate PRE word.**

1. The dot.com failure was _____ by the sudden fall in investor confidence.

2. She insisted that her child was _____ because of her early drawing ability.

3. The court decision set a _____ that was followed for many years.

4. I have a _____ for blue and find it hard to buy any other color.

5. His strong stand against forced retirement was _____ in that company. No one had ever taken such a stand before.

6. After publishing her research, she was considered _____ in her field.

7. Most professional writers strive to use _____ language.

8. The _____ to the club's constitution also explained its mission.

9. Most of us are _____ in some ways against those we do not know.

10. The U.S. military _____ in World War II.

11. The ability to drive a tractor is a _____ for the job.

12. The _____ to the symphony was euphonious.

13. The _____ message by the oil companies is that they are not to blame for the rising oil prices.

14. Good stories include foreshadowing, and often as a reader you can _____ the outcome.

✎ EXERCISE 2 **Remember to add words to your WORD LIST after each session. Try to use a few of these words in conversation each day.**

PRO—forward, before, for, forth

Do you tend to put off unpleasant tasks until a future time? If so, you probably have a **propensity** [PRO forward + PENS to hang] (a hanging *forward* or inclination) to **procrastinate** [PRO forward + CRAS tomorrow] (to push tasks *forward* until tomorrow). When it comes to studying, many students have a propensity to procrastinate.

proceed (pro sēd') [PRO forward + CEED to go]—to go forward. *Now that the members are all here, the meeting will proceed.*

proclaim (pro klām') [PRO forth + CLAM to cry out]—to announce officially and publicly. *The day was proclaimed a holiday.*

proclivity (pro kliv' uh tē) [PRO forward + CLIVUS slope]—*lit.* a slope forward; an inclination toward something, especially toward something objectionable. *Her proclivity to exaggerate finally led to her losing her job.*

procrastinate (pro kras' tuh nāt) [PRO forward + CRAS tomorrow]—*lit.* to push forward until tomorrow; to put off doing something until a future time. *I always procrastinate about cleaning the house.*

profuse (pruh fyOs') [PRO forth + FUS to pour]—pouring forth freely; generous. *The mechanic was profuse in her apologies.*

profusion (pruh fyO' zhun) [PRO forth + FUS to pour]—*lit.* a pouring forth; an abundance. *The profusion of wildflowers on the hill delighted us.*

projectile (pruh jek' tīl) [PRO forward + JECT to throw]—something thrown forward by force; a missile. *The projectile just missed a populated area.*

promontory (prom' un tor ē) [PRO forward + MONT mountain]—a high peak of land or rock (mountain) jutting forward into the sea. *From the promontory, we had a view of the entire area.*

promotion (pruh mo' shun) [PRO forward + MOT to move]—a moving forward, as to a better job. *My sister is hoping for a promotion.*

propel (pruh pel') [PRO forward + PEL to push]—to push or drive forward. *Against his wishes, he was propelled into the race.*

propensity (pruh pen' suh tē) [PRO forward + PENS to hang]—*lit.* a hanging forward; a natural inclination. *He has a propensity for putting things off.* (Propensity and proclivity are close synonyms.)

proponent (pruh po' nunt) [PRO before + PON to put]—*lit.* one who puts something before people; one who argues in favor of something; an advocate. *A leading proponent of recycling is speaking tonight.*

prospectus (pruh spek' tus) [PRO forward + SPECT to look]—*lit.* a looking forward; a printed description of a proposed enterprise. *The prospectus made the new subdivision look inviting.*

protuberant (pro tO' bur unt) [PRO forth + TUBER swelling]—bulging. *From childhood he had been conscious of his protuberant nose.*

provident (prov' uh dunt) [PRO before + VID to see]—*lit.* seeing beforehand; making provision for the future. *If he had been more provident, he wouldn't be in need now.*

provision (pruh vizh' un) [PRO before + VIS to see]—a seeing beforehand; a preparation for the future. *The parents had made provisions for their son's college expenses.*

ALSO: improvise, proclamation, produce, progenitor, progeny, prognosis, prognosticate, program, prologue, promulgate, pronoun, prophet, propitiate, propitious, proscribe, protracted, provide, provocation

EXERCISE 1   Write the appropriate PRO word.

1. The _____ for the investment fund was tempting.
2. His _____ or _____ for wasting time may cost him his job.
3. She's a _____ of the amendment to ban disposable bottles.
4. All his children inherited his _____ ears.
5. Whenever I _____, someone always quotes the old epigram, "Don't put off until tomorrow . . . ."
6. His tardiness was always followed by a _____ of excuses.
7. We stood on the _____ and looked out over the ocean.
8. Always a _____ person, he had taken care of his family's needs before he left for the month.
9. With _____ thanks, she accepted the award.
10. Accused rapist Caryl Chessman _____ his innocence.
11. My hard work _____ me to a _____ at work.

EXERCISE 2 JOURNAL   In your *vocabulary journal*, write a humorous paragraph using as many PRO and PRE words as possible.

EXERCISE 3 REVIEW   Match each word root with its meaning.

1. _____ PHIL   **A.** after
2. _____ PHOB   **B.** forward, before, for, forth
3. _____ PHON   **C.** before
4. _____ POST   **D.** to love
5. _____ PRE   **E.** sound
6. _____ PRO   **F.** fear

RE—back, again

What would you do with a recalcitrant child? First you might have to figure out the meaning of **recalcitrant**. Since RE means *back* and CALC means *heel,* recalcitrant means literally kicking *back* the heels. Once used in referring to horses and mules, it now is applied to human beings. Therefore a recalcitrant child would be one who is kicking *back,* obstinate, stubbornly rebellious.

The meaning of many words that begin with RE are simple: **return** is simply to turn *again,* **recall** is to call *again,* and **reconstruct** is to construct *again.* Here are some more familiar words for which you won't need pronunciation help or example sentences.

recede [RE back + CED to go]—to go back, as a river recedes from its banks.

receive [RE again + CAP to take]—*lit.* to take again; to take something offered.

recreation [RE again + CREAT to create]—*lit.* a creating again; the refreshment of mind or body through some form of play or amusement.

referee [RE back + FER to carry]—one to whom questions are carried back; an official in a sports contest.

remit [RE back + MIT to send]—to send back, as to remit payment.

reside [RE back + SID to sit]—*lit.* to sit back; to dwell, as to reside in a house.

residue [RE back + SID to sit]—*lit.* that which sits back; the part that remains after part has been separated away, as the residue in the bottom of a vase.

retain [RE back + TEN to hold]—to hold back or keep in one's possession.

revenue [RE back + VEN to come]—money that comes back from an investment or other source; taxes and other income collected by a government.

revise [RE again + VIS to see]—to see again in order to correct errors.

revive [RE again + VIV to live]—to cause to live again.

And here are some less familiar words.

recalcitrant (ri kal' suh trunt) [RE back + CALC heel]—*lit.* kicking back the heels; obstinate; stubbornly rebellious. *It's useless to argue with her when she's in a recalcitrant mood.*

recant (ri kant') [RE back + CANT to sing]—to renounce a belief formerly held, especially in a formal or public manner. *The judge chose to recant publicly his former stand on capital punishment.*

recession (ri sesh' un) [RE back + CESS to go]—a period of reduced economic activity. *The government feared a business recession.*

recluse (rek' lOs) [RE back + CLUS to shut]—one who lives shut back from the world. *The poet Emily Dickinson lived as a recluse in her house in Amherst.*

remiss (ri mis') [RE back + MISS to send]—*lit.* sent back; negligent; lax in attending to duty. *I've been remiss about doing my exercises.*

remission (ri mish' un) [RE back + MISS to send]—*lit.* a sending back; a lessening, as a remission of disease; forgiveness, as remission of sins. *He enjoyed periods of remission from his illness.*

Renaissance (ren' uh sahns) [RE again + NASC to be born]—a rebirth; the revival of classical art, literature, and learning in Europe in the fourteenth, fifteenth, and sixteenth centuries. *Michelangelo was an artist of the Renaissance.*

resilience (ri zil' yunts) [RE again + SIL to leap]—*lit.* to leap again; the ability to recover quickly
from illness, change, or misfortune. *With her customary resilience, she bounced back after
her long illness.*

revert (ri vurt') [RE back + VERT to turn]—*lit.* to turn back; to return to a former habit or
condition. *Occasionally, she would revert to her childhood dialect.*

ALSO: irrevocable, rebel, recapitulate, reclaim, recourse, recur, recurrent, reflect, refractory, reject,
repel, respect, retort, revoke, revolve

EXERCISE 1   Write the appropriate RE word.

1. They were afraid to make any investments for fear there would be a _____.

2. He had never been an unruly or _____ child.

3. Occasionally, however, he would _____ to infant behavior.

4. One needs plenty of _____ to cope with all the disappointments
in that job.

5. She had a few weeks of good health during a _____ of her illness.

6. Living like a _____, he avoids all social contacts.

7. The best French and Italian painters emerged during the _____
period.

8. The candidate has taken such a strong stand that for him to _____
would be unthinkable.

9. The accountant was _____ at filing his own tax return and had
to pay a late fee to the IRS.

10. She argued with the _____ student over his behavior.

11. My writing teacher reminded me that to _____ means to
remember.

12. Laura reminded us that we need _____ as well as work.

13. We had to _____ the payment in full before they would let us
take the furniture.

14. The school decided to _____ the Latin courses after an absence
of ten years.

15. She will _____ the receipt in case she wants to return the item.

✎ **EXERCISE 2 REVIEW**   Write C in front of each sentence in which all words are used correctly. Then, in each remaining blank, write the word that should have been used.

1. _____ Deciding to emigrate from their homeland, they moved to Canada.

2. _____ Federal laws are attempting to eradicate sexual discrimination.

3. _____ They watched the smokestack emit pollutants.

4. _____ She embroidered her monograph on all her towels.

5. _____ The public was becoming aware of the demagoguery in the mayor's speeches.

6. _____ You can count on his resilience to help him make a comeback even when he loses.

7. _____ We were amazed at the profusion of flowers in their garden.

8. _____ She decided to take a course in astrology at the university.

9. _____ The antiquarian bookseller has an amazing collection of early Postimpressionist books.

10. _____ Some speakers are quite unconcerned with their diction and sometimes speak unclearly.

✎ **EXERCISE 3 REVIEW**   Using the following 12 words, fill in the blanks in the paragraph so that it makes sense. After you check your answers in the back of the book, reread the paragraph and see how satisfying it is to read a paragraph in which you are sure of all the words.

discomfited	diffident	amorphous	current
presages	credible	profusely	etymology
addict	ebullient	recourse	precise

I've read that a large vocabulary _____ success both in college and in one's career. The idea sounds _____, and I'm now taking more interest in _____. I've become a real word _____ and am no longer _____ about using new words. Sometimes my friends are _____ by my new hobby, but gradually even they are discovering the _____ feeling that comes from using _____ words.

✎ **EXERCISE 4 REVIEW**   Here, taken from magazine articles, are sentences containing words you have studied. Underline the appropriate review word in each sentence and provide its meaning. Check in the Word Index for any words you don't remember.

1. St. Augustine, Florida, boasts it is the oldest city in the United States; many of its homes antedate the Revolutionary War.

2. The British prime minister excoriated the new Labour Party leaders.

3. Concerning his first experience with weightlessness, the astronaut said, "I was in an almost euphoric condition."

4. The president of the United Nations Security Council engendered the respect of the African delegation.

5. Gregory Hines highlighted the dance's meaning with a panoply of foot moves.

6. The deadly plague reached across the Mediterranean from Africa during the first pandemic, beginning in A.D. 541.

7. The senator predicts that gas prices will remain high.

8. The student's propensity to analyze literature is admirable.

9. The success of the government's economic programs has also given rise to unprecedented problems.

10. The FCC's report contained a cacophony of conflicting claims, bewildering investors.

11. Two hundred researchers from nine countries meeting in Snowmass, Colorado, reached a consensus: CFCs are causing the gaps in the ozone layer.

12. The bumpy road forced us to proceed with caution to the backwater town.

13. The doctor noted that more boys than girls are diagnosed with hyperactivity by their teachers.

14. Often the starting salary is not commensurate with the experience of the job candidate.

15. Geometry is now being introduced to middle school students.

✎ **EXERCISE 5**   Remember to add words to your WORD LIST after each session. Try to use a few of these words in conversation each day.

SCRIB, SCRIPT—to write

In Europe during the fifth century, a monk copied a manuscript, thus becoming the first European **scribe**. Before long, entire monasteries were devoted to copying scriptural and literary texts. The scribes copied the texts laboriously in black, glossy letters; then other monks illuminated the capital letters with red pigment and gold leaf. Sometimes the making of a single book would occupy many years or even the lifetime of a monk.

ascribe (uh skrīb′) [AD to + SCRIB to write]—*lit.* to write to; to attribute. *His parents ascribed his actions to his eagerness to succeed.*

conscription (kun skrip′ shun) [CON together + SCRIPT to write]—*lit.* names written together; an enforced enrollment or military draft. *Conscription was often necessary to provide a large army.*

inscribe (in skrīb′) [IN in + SCRIB to write]—originally, to engrave words in stone; now, to write in, as the dedication of a book. *The author inscribed my copy of her book.*

manuscript (man′ yuh skript) [MANU hand + SCRIPT to write]—originally, something written by hand; now, a composition for publication. *He sent his manuscript to the publisher.*

nondescript (non′ di skript) [NON not + SCRIPT to write]—not easy to write about or describe, lacking in distinctive qualities. *Even though her outfit was nondescript, she was still the most striking person in the room.*

prescribe (pri skrīb′) [PRE before + SCRIB to write]—to write down a rule beforehand; in medicine, to order a treatment. *The doctor prescribed an antibiotic.*

proscribe (pro skrīb′) [PRO before + SCRIB to write]—in ancient Rome, to publish the name of one condemned to death; now, to condemn or forbid as harmful. *Some religions proscribe abortion.*

scribe (skrīb)—one who copies manuscripts. *In ancient Israel, the scribes copied the Scriptures.*

script (skript)—handwriting; also, the written copy of a play used by actors to learn their lines. *She was studying the script for her part in the play.*

Scripture (skrip′ chur)—originally, anything written; now, the Bible. *The library owns the King James version of the Scripture.*

subscribe (sub skrīb′) [SUB under + SCRIB to write]—to write one's name on an agreement, as to subscribe to a magazine; also, to support or give approval to an idea. *Congress subscribed to the foreign policy of the president.*

transcribe (tran skrīb′) [TRANS over + SCRIB to write]—to write over again, as to transcribe notes. *After taking dictation in shorthand, he immediately transcribed his notes on the word processor.*

ALSO: circumscribe, describe, postscript, scribble, subscription, transcript

✎ **EXERCISE 1**   Write the appropriate SCRIB, SCRIPT word.

1. They will probably _____ the failure of their plan to lack of funds.

2. His clothes were always _____ and unpressed.

3. It's wise to _____ one's class notes immediately after taking them.

4. During times of peace, _____ is unnecessary.

5. Do you _____ to new ideas?

6. The court has _____ racial discrimination in housing.

✎ **EXERCISE 2 REVIEW**   Write C in front of each sentence in which all words are used correctly.

1. _____ The ancient Roman belief in many gods is called pantheism.

2. _____ The proponents of the metric system are trying to bring the United States into line with the rest of the world.

3. _____ Because her parents had not been provident, she was never in want.

4. _____ The prospectus for the new housing development made us want to move there.

5. _____ To procrastinate about doing an unpleasant task is simply to postpone it.

6. _____ The Impressionists came before the Postimpressionists.

7. _____ The captain had set a precedent of fair play that his teammates now followed.

8. _____ The Renaissance in Italy was a revolt of the common people.

9. _____ Because she was ambidextrous, she had to travel in a wheelchair.

10. _____ From the top floor of the building, we could see the panorama of the entire countryside.

11. _____ The child's fear of the dark has become a phobia.

12. _____ No one has ever doubted the credibility of our governor.

13. _____ The batter was always tempted to revert to his old way of hitting the ball.

14. _____ Television was the precursor of radio.

15. _____ It was pleasant to watch the play in the outdoor amphitheater.

16. _____ Her excellent vocabulary was an impediment to her reading.

17. _____ They celebrated their centennial wedding anniversary when they had been married 50 years.

18. _____ "Lots of kids flunked" is a colloquial expression for "Many students failed."

SED, SID, SESS—to sit

If you have a **sedentary** job, you probably *sit* at a desk all day. If you work **assiduously**, you literally *sit* at your work until it is finished. And if you have an **insidious** habit, it is one that does not seem very bad at first but that *sits* in wait for you, ready to become more and more harmful.

assess (uh ses´) [AD to + SESS to sit]—*lit.* to sit near to a judge (as an assistant); to estimate the value of property for taxation. *Their property was assessed at a higher rate than formerly.*

assessor (uh ses´ ur) [AD to + SESS to sit]—*lit.* one who sits near to a judge as an assistant; an official who assesses property for taxation. *They were waiting for the assessor to evaluate their new home.*

assiduous (uh sij´ O us)—*lit.* sitting at something until it is finished; persistent. *The new clerk was assiduous in performing all his duties.*

insidious (in sid´ ē us) [IN in + SID to sit]—*lit.* sitting in wait for; treacherous, more dangerous than seems evident. *Malaria is an insidious disease, remaining in the body ready to strike again and again.*

obsess (ub ses´) [OB against + SESS to sit]—*lit.* to sit against; to besiege like an evil spirit; to preoccupy the mind abnormally. *He was obsessed with the fear of failure.*

obsession (ub sesh´ un) [OB against + SESS to sit]—originally, the act of an evil spirit in ruling (sitting against) one; now, a persistent idea, desire, or emotion that cannot be got rid of by reasoning. *Her desire to act in movies had become an obsession.*

preside (pri zīd´) [PRE before + SID to sit]—*lit.* to sit before a meeting to conduct it. *The vice president had to preside in the president's absence.*

president (prez´ ud unt) [PRE before + SID to sit]—*lit.* one who sits before a group as its head. *We waited for the president to state his views.*

sedative (sed´ uh tiv)—*lit.* a medicine that makes one sit down or quiet down; a medicine that calms nervousness or excitement. *The doctor prescribed a sedative to calm him.*

sedentary (sed´ n ter ē)—requiring much sitting. *Because he had a sedentary job, he didn't get enough exercise.*

sediment (sed´ uh munt)—material that sits at the bottom of a liquid, as the sediment in a stream. *We noted the sediment in the bottom of the glass.*

session (sesh´ un)—the sitting together of a group. *School is in session now.*

siege (sēj)—*lit.* sitting down before a town with the intention of capturing it; a prolonged attack, as of illness. *She had a siege of flu that lasted all winter.*

subside (sub sīd´) [SUB under + SID to sit]—*lit.* to sit under; to sink to a lower level; to settle down. *After midnight, the noise subsided.*

subsidiary (sub sid´ ē er ē) [SUB under + SID to sit]—*lit.* sitting under; serving to assist or supplement; subordinate. *The company had several subsidiary branches.*

subsidy (sub´ suh dē) [SUB under + SID to sit]—*lit.* sitting under prices to hold them up; government financial support. *When corn prices were low, the farmers received a subsidy.*

supersede (sO pur sēd´) [SUPER above + SED to sit]—*lit.* to sit above; to take the place of; to displace. *Solar heating is superseding other forms of heating in many areas.*

ALSO: dissident, reside, residue, sedan

✎ **EXERCISE 1**   Write the appropriate SED, SID, SESS word.

1. A(n) _____ occupation has never appealed to her because she doesn't like to sit still.

2. Nevertheless, she was a(n) _____ worker, doing the job to the best of her ability.

3. The government _____ to farmers was cut back during the Depression.

4. The chemicals had a(n) _____ effect on the stream, the real damage not showing up for months.

5. The complaints of the environmentalists about the pollution did not _____ when the election was over.

6. The computer has _____ the typewriter.

7. Having everything immaculate is a(n) _____ with her.

8. The company's _____ branches were located overseas, where labor was cheaper.

9. Becoming _____ with a desire to win, he thought of nothing else.

10. What he has done for the school is so important that it would be difficult to _____ its value.

11. The county _____ evaluated their land.

12. During the Middle Ages, enemies laid _____ against each other by fighting continuous battles.

13. Ellen's doctor prescribed a _____ after the traumatic experience.

14. The U.S. president _____ over the military

15. The instructor assured us that each _____ of class was sure to be interesting.

16. The _____ at the bottom of the lake squished between our toes.

✎ **EXERCISE 2 JOURNAL**   In your *vocabulary journal,* write several sentences about a writing project you've done. Use as many SED, SID, SESS, SCRIB, and SCRIPT words as possible.

SPEC, SPIC, SPECT—to look

In ancient Rome, certain men were appointed to *look* at the flight of birds for omens or signs. The kind of birds, their position in the sky, and the direction of their flight determined whether the time was **auspicious** [AVI bird + SPIC to look] for any new undertaking. **Auspicious** came to mean "full of good omens," and today we still speak of an auspicious time to ask a favor or to suggest a new policy.

aspect (as´ pekt) [AD to + SPECT to look]—the way something looks from a certain point of view. *He was concerned about another aspect of the case.*

auspicious (aw spish´ us) [AVI bird + SPIC to look]—originally, looking at the flight of birds for omens; today, promising good luck; favorable. *It wasn't an auspicious time to ask for a raise.*

conspicuous (kun spik´ yuh wus) [CON (intensive) + SPIC to look]—easy to notice (look at); obvious. *Her late arrival made her conspicuous.*

despicable (duh spik´ uh bul) [DE down + SPIC to look]—looked down on; deserving to be despised; contemptible. *Reading someone else's mail is despicable.*

inspect (in spekt´) [IN into + SPECT to look]—to look into carefully. *We waited for the border guard to inspect our luggage.*

introspection (in truh spek´ shun) [INTRO within + SPECT to look]—a looking within one's own mind. *Introspection was valuable in helping her solve some of her problems.*

perspective (pur spek´ tiv) [PER through + SPECT to look]—the ability to look at things in their true relationship; point of view. *Whether you consider the difficulty insurmountable depends on your perspective.*

perspicacious (per spi kā´ shus) [PER through + SPIC to look]—having the ability to look through something and understand it; perceptive. *In dealing with individual employee problems, he was exceptionally perspicacious.*

prospect (prah´ spekt) [PRO forward + SPECT to look]—a looking forward; the outlook for something, as a prospect for a good crop. *The prospect for lower taxes is slim.*

respect (ri spekt´) [RE again + SPECT to look]—*lit.* to look on again; to look on with regard or esteem. *We have the greatest respect for our leader.*

retrospect (ret´ ruh spekt) [RETRO backward + SPECT to look]—a looking backward. *In retrospect, his life did not seem so unhappy.*

specious (spē´ shus)—looking good on first sight but actually not so. *It was hard not to be taken in by the specious advertising for the baldness remedy.*

specter (spec´ tur)—a mental image that looks real; a ghost; any object of fear or dread. *Her father was troubled by the specter of unemployment.*

spectrum (spek´ trum)—a series of colored bands seen when light passes through a prism. *All the colors of the spectrum were included in her painting.* Also, a broad range of ideas or activities. *His interests included the entire spectrum of the arts.*

speculate (spek´ yuh lāt)—*lit.* to look at; to reflect on or ponder. *The candidate speculated on his chances of winning.*

ALSO: circumspect, expect, inauspicious, introspective, perspicacity, prospective, prospector, prospectus, respectable, retrospection, species, specific, specimen, spectacle, spectacles, spectacular, spectator, suspect, suspicious

EXERCISE 1   Write the appropriate SPEC, SPIC, SPECT word.

1. The failure of the first project was not a(n) _____ start for the coming year.

2. The salesperson could see the problem from the customer's _____.

3. She enjoyed living those years again in _____.

4. He examined his motives in a moment of quiet _____.

5. Cheating the person who had befriended him was _____.

6. The professor was unusually _____ in analyzing the problems of the students.

7. The _____ advertising made the car deal look like a giveaway.

8. One experiences the entire _____ of emotions watching that play.

9. The _____ of failure haunted her.

10. The golf pro wouldn't _____ on the outcome of the U.S. Open.

EXERCISE 2 REVIEW   Match each word with its definition.

A. protuberant	**D.** apathy	**G.** metamorphosis	**I.** malaise
B. bibliophile	**E.** loquacious	**H.** missive	**J.** epigram
C. monarchy	**F.** perfidious		

1. _____ government with one hereditary ruler

2. _____ bulging

3. _____ one who loves books

4. _____ talkative

5. _____ lack of feeling; indifference

6. _____ deceiving through pretense of faith; treacherous

7. _____ the ability to change form or shape

8. _____ vague feeling of illness or depression

9. _____ letter or message sent

10. _____ writing on any subject; short witty saying

SUB—under

Prisoners in Roman times were forced to crawl *under* a yoke (like the yoke put on oxen) formed from three spears, thus showing that from that time forward they were the subjects of their conquerors. They were brought *under* (SUB) the yoke (JUGUM) or **subjugated**. We still use the word **subjugate** today to mean subdue or make **subservient**.

Many SUB words are easy to understand when we know that SUB means *under:* **subcommittee**, **subconscious**, **subcontractor**, **subculture**, **subnormal**, **substandard**, and **subway**. But SUB can also help clarify the meaning of some less common words such as **subliminal** and **subsume**.

subject (accent on last syllable) (sub jekt´) [SUB under + JECT to throw]—*lit.* to throw under the influence of; to submit to the authority of, as to subject oneself to a strict diet. *She learned to subject herself to the office routine.*

  (There is also, of course, **subject** with the accent on the first syllable. *Her favorite subject is math.*)

subjugate (sub´ juh gāt) [SUB under + JUGUM a yoke]—*lit.* to place under a yoke; to conquer. *The invaders subjugated the primitive tribe.*

subliminal (sub lim´ uh nul) [SUB under + LIMIN threshold]—below the threshold of conscious perception. *The popcorn ad flashed on the theater screen too briefly to be seen consciously, but it had a subliminal effect—people immediately started going to the lobby for popcorn.*

submerge (sub murj´) [SUB under + MERG to plunge]—to plunge under water. *I learned to swim a few strokes when completely submerged.*

submit (sub mit´) [SUB under + MIT to send]—to put (send) oneself under the authority of. *I had to submit to the rules.*

subpoena (suh pē´ nuh) [SUB under + POENA penalty (the first two words of the order)]—a legal order requiring a person to appear in court to give testimony. *She received a subpoena to appear in court the next week.*

sub rosa (sub ro´ zuh) [SUB under + ROS rose]—*lit.* under the rose (from an ancient custom of hanging a rose over the council table to indicate that all present were sworn to secrecy); in confidence. *In the interview, the president was speaking sub rosa.*

subservient (sub sur´ vē unt) [SUB under + SERV to serve]—*lit.* serving under someone; submissive, as a servant might be. *His attitude toward his superiors was always subservient.*

subsistence (sub sis´ tunts)—*lit.* underexistence; the barest means to sustain life. *They had barely enough food for subsistence.*

subsume (sub sOm´) [SUB under + SUM to take]—to include under a more general category. *The three minor rules are subsumed under the major one.*

subterfuge (sub´ tur fyOj) [SUB under + FUG to flee]—*lit.* fleeing under cover; an action used to avoid an unpleasant situation. *By using the subterfuge of having to work overtime, he avoided going to the meeting.*

subterranean (sub tuh ra´ nē un) [SUB under + TERR earth]—under the surface of the Earth. *Subterranean remains of an early civilization were found on the island.*

subversive (sub vur´ siv) [SUB under + VERS to turn]—*lit.* to turn under; tending to undermine or overthrow. *The government was threatened by subversive groups.*

ALSO: subcutaneous, subjective, submarine, submit, subordinate, subscribe, subsequent, subside, subsidy, subtle, suburb, suffuse, surreptitious

✎ **EXERCISE 1**   Write the appropriate SUB word.

1. He was completely _____ by the giant wave.

2. The prison inmates were _____ to strict rules.

3. With such a low-paying job, he and his family lived at a _____ level.

4. The dictator was trying to quell the _____ forces in the country.

5. She thought of a clever _____ to get out of doing the job.

6. He was so _____ that he never objected to his supervisor's unreasonable demands.

7. The superpower was trying to _____ all the small nations around it.

8. A person can be influenced not only in conscious ways but also in _____ ways.

9. All his arguments can be _____ in a summarized document.

10. The driver of the other car received a _____ to appear in court as a witness.

11. Bats flew out of the _____ cave.

12. Unwilling to have his remarks published, the dean asked that they be considered _____.

13. The rebellious teenager did not want to _____ to the school's regulations.

✎ **EXERCISE 2 JOURNAL**   In your *vocabulary journal,* write several sentences using as many SUB words as possible.

SUPER—above, over

How do you describe people who raise their eyebrows and look down on others in a haughty way? Two roots—SUPER *above* and CILIUM *eyelid*—combined to form the Latin word *supercilium* meaning eyebrow. Eventually, anyone who raised their eyebrows in a haughty way came to be called a **supercilious** person, a raised-eyebrows person.

insuperable (in sO´ pur uh bul) [IN not + SUPER over]—not capable of being overcome. *His height was an insuperable barrier to his becoming a jockey.*

soprano (su pran´ ō)—one having a voice range above other voices. *Her soprano solo won top honors.*

superb (su purb´)—above ordinary quality; excellent. *That was a superb performance.*

supercilious (sO pur sil´ e us) [SUPER above + CILIUM eyelid]—*lit.* above the eyelid; eyebrows raised in a haughty way. *She cast a supercilious glance at the person who had dared to disagree with her.*

superfluous (su pur´ fO wus) [SUPER over + FLU to flow]—*lit.* overflowing what is needed; extra. *The essay was full of superfluous words.*

superimpose (sO pur im poz´)—to lay something over something else. *The modern painting had been superimposed on an old masterpiece.*

superior (su pir´ e ur)—above others. *Our home team was superior.*

supernumerary (sO pur nO´ muh rer ē) [SUPER above + NUMER number]—someone in excess of (above) the number required; an extra. *Since she was given no work to do, she felt like a supernumerary.* Also, a performer in the theater without a speaking part. *He was a supernumerary in the mob scene.*

supersonic (sO pur son´ ik) [SUPER above + SON sound]—above the speed of sound. *Supersonic planes cause the sound known as sonic boom.*

superstition (sO pur stish´ un) [SUPER above + STA to stand]—*lit.* a belief standing above other beliefs; a belief that is inconsistent with the known laws of science. *Believing that the number 13 is unlucky is a superstition.*

supervise (sO´ pur vīz) [SUPER over + VIS to see]—to oversee others. *She will supervise the preschoolers.*

supervisor (sO´ pur vīz zur) [SUPER over + VIS to see]—one who oversees others. *She is the supervisor of the preschool.*

supreme (su prēm´)—above all others; highest in rank. *He considers himself the supreme authority in that company.*

surplus (sur´ plus) [SUPER above + PLUS more]—*lit.* above more; above what is needed. *We have a surplus of volunteers.*

ALSO: superabundant, superannuated, superhuman, superintend, supernatural, supersede

✎ **EXERCISE 1**   Which SUPER word names or describes the following?

1. above the speed of sound   _____
2. more than is needed   _____
3. to lay something over something else _____
4. incapable of being overcome   _____
5. haughty   _____

✎ **EXERCISE 2**   Fill in the correct SUPER word.

1. My grandmother believed every _____, especially about breaking mirrors causing bad luck.
2. It takes a watchful eye to _____ a class five-year-olds on the
   playground.
3. The solid oak desk was of _____ quality as compared to the one
   made of pressed woodchips.
4. Thousands of Confederate and Union soldiers gave the _____ sac-
   rifice fighting for their beliefs.
5. The _____ singer in our chorus has a light, pretty voice.
6. The _____ wine won numerous awards.
7. Alexis's _____ comments added an extra hour to the meeting.
8. The fledging actor was happy just to get the _____ role in the
   movie.
9. Her promotion made her the _____ of several departments.
10. The restaurant donated the _____ food to the poor.

✎ **EXERCISE 3 REVIEW**   As a review of the words you've been studying, read these
paragraphs. How many of the ten underlined words do you know without looking them
up? Add any you are unsure of to your WORD LIST.

A town meeting was called to consider a lumber company's proposal to cut trees in a town-
owned woodland. The <u>proponents</u> of the plan claimed it would create jobs and bring
<u>unprecedented</u> wealth to the town, which was in <u>chronic</u> economic depression. They said that
those trying to <u>circumvent</u> the plan were asking for the <u>demise</u> of the community.

   Those interested in <u>ecology</u>, on the other hand, said that the natural beauty of the area would
be spoiled and that several <u>endemic</u> plants might become extinct. It isn't possible, they said, to
<u>equate</u> financial gain with the good life.

   The problem seemed <u>insuperable</u> because after three hours of discussion, no <u>consensus</u> was
reached.

SYN, SYM, SYL—together, with

Among the ancient Greeks, a **symposium** was a *drinking together* party [SYM together + POS to drink], especially after a banquet. Through the years, the meaning has changed until today a symposium is no longer a drinking party but a meeting or conference at which several speakers come *together* to deliver opinions on a certain topic.

In preceding pages, we have seen that the root SYN, SYM, SYL means *together* in such words as **symmetrical**, **sympathy**, **symphony**, and **synchronize**. Whether the word will begin with SYN, SYM, or SYL often depends on what letter follows. For instance, it would be difficult to pronounce SYNmetrical; therefore SYN becomes SYM. For more about how a root may change one of its letters for easier pronunciation, see page 6.

syllogism (sil' uh jiz um) [SYL together + LOG word]—*lit.* words together; a form of argument or reasoning consisting of two statements and a conclusion drawn from them. *Here is an example of a syllogism: All mammals are warm-blooded; whales are mammals; therefore whales are warm-blooded.*

symbol (sim' bul) [SYM together + BOL to throw]—*lit.* things thrown together for comparison; something that represents something else. *Diamonds are a symbol of wealth.*

symposium (sim po' zee um) [SYM together + POS to drink]—originally, a drinking (together) party following a banquet among the early Greeks; now, a meeting at which several speakers deliver opinions on a certain topic. *A symposium on the use of national parks was held in Washington, D.C.*

synagogue (sin' u gahg) [SYN together + AGOG to lead]—a place where Jews come together for worship. *We visited an architecturally famous synagogue in Elkins Park, Pennsylvania.*

syndrome (sin' drōm) [SYN together + DROM to run]—*lit.* a running together; a group of symptoms that run together and indicate a specific disease or condition. *He had the usual flu syndrome: sore throat, headache, and aching muscles.*

synergistic (sin ur jis' tik) [SYN together + ERG work]—working together, as when the joint action of two drugs increases the effectiveness of each. *Certain drugs are synergistic when taken together. The two playwrights had a synergistic relationship, each working more effectively when they worked together.*

synod (sin' ud) [SYN together + OD road, journey]—*lit.* a journey together; a council or assembly, especially of church officials. *The church synod met in a different city each year.*

synopsis (su nahp' sus) [SYN together + OP sight]—*lit.* a seeing things together; a brief general summary. *Before beginning our study of the novel, we read a synopsis of it.*

syntax (sin' tax) [SYN together + TAX arrangement]—the way words are arranged together to form sentences. *Because English was a second language for her, she often had trouble with syntax.* Also, in computer science, the rules governing the construction of any computer language. *The computer kept responding, "Syntax error."*

synthesis (sin' thuh sis) [SYN together + THES to put]—*lit.* a putting together; the combining of separate elements into a whole. *Sandburg said that poetry is a synthesis of hyacinths and biscuits.*

synthetic (sin thet' ik) [SYN together + THET to put]—*lit.* put together; produced by putting separate elements together; artificial. *Instead of a synthetic cloth, she wanted a natural fiber, such as silk or cotton.*

ALSO: asymmetric, photosynthesis, symbiosis, symbiotic, symmetrical, sympathy, symphony, synchronize, synergy, synonym

EXERCISE 1   **Write the appropriate SYN, SYM, SYL word.**

1. The final motion was a _____ of all their ideas.

2. Six speakers were scheduled for the _____ on air pollution.

3. _____ cloth is made by combining various chemical elements.

4. The diagnosis was simple because the child had the typical chickenpox _____.

5. The matter was discussed at the annual meeting of the church _____.

6. Because he had never paid any attention to grammar in high school, he now had difficulty using correct _____ in his writing.

7. Learning the correct form for a _____ helped her to think logically.

8. She and her husband had a _____ relationship, each working better on the project when they worked together.

9. In an early chapter of *The Grapes of Wrath*, Steinbeck uses a turtle as a _____ of the migrants.

10. Jews pray in a _____, Muslims pray in a mosque, and Hindus pray in a temple.

✎ **EXERCISE 2 REVIEW**   Give the meaning of each root and a word in which it is found.

ROOT	MEANING	WORD
1. A, AN		
2. ANTHROP		
3. ANTI		
4. AUTO		
5. BENE		
6. CEDE		
7. COM, CON, COL, COR		
8. CUR		
9. DICT		
10. DIS, DI, DIF		
11. EQU		
12. EU		
13. EX, ES, E		
14. FID		
15. GEN		
16. GRAPH, GRAM		
17. HYPER		
18. LOG		
19. -LOGY		
20. LOQU, LOC		
21. MAL		
22. METER, METR		
23. MIT, MIS, MISS		
24. MONO		
25. MORPH		
26. PAN		

ROOT	MEANING	WORD
27. PATH	_____	_____
28. PED	_____	_____
29. PHIL	_____	_____
30. PHOB	_____	_____
31. PHON	_____	_____
32. POST	_____	_____
33. PRE	_____	_____
34. PRO	_____	_____
35. RE	_____	_____
36. SCRIB, SCRIPT	_____	_____
37. SED, SID, SESS	_____	_____
38. SPEC, SPIC, SPECT	_____	_____

TELE—far

Any word containing TELE will have *far* in its meaning. Such words as **telephone, telegraph,** and **television** have become so common that we say them without thinking about what they really mean.

telegraph (tel′ uh graf) [TELE far + GRAPH to write]—*lit.* an instrument for (far) writing; a system for transmitting messages by electric impulses sent through a wire or converted into radio waves. *Western Union offices were originally called telegraph offices.*

telemetry (tuh lem′ uh trē) [TELE far + METER measure]—the automatic measurement and transmission of data by radio from far away, as from space vehicles to a receiving station. *Reports of the weather on Mars came to the research center in California by telemetry.*

telepathy (tuh lep′ uh thē) [TELE far + PATH feeling]—*lit.* far feeling; the supposed communication between two people far apart by other than normal sensory means. *Because they so often thought of the same thing at the same time, they were convinced it was telepathy.*

telephone (tel′ uh fōn) [TELE far + PHON sound]—an instrument for transmitting sounds from far away. *Alexander Graham Bell invented the telephone.*

telescope (tel′ uh skōp) [TELE far + SCOP to look]—an instrument for looking at far objects. *We looked at the moon through a telescope.*

television (tel′ uh vizh un) [TELE far + VIS to see]—an instrument for seeing images from afar. *Television was unknown in the first part of the twentieth century.*

ALSO: telecommunication, telegram, telephoto

EXERCISE 1   Write the appropriate TELE word.

1. _____ is used by astronomers and astrophysicists.
2. There are several ways to see the universe; the best is through a _____.
3. Deborah wants to believe that the astrologer used _____ to "contact" her deceased father.
4. The _____ and _____ changed the way we interact with one another.

EXERCISE 2 REVIEW   Match the word to its definition

1. _____ superfluous
2. _____ perspicacious
3. _____ assiduous
4. _____ proscribe
5. _____ recalcitrant

A. persistent
B. condemn or forbid as harmful
C. stubbornly rebellious
D. overflowing what is needed; extra
E. having the ability to look through something and understand it; perceptive

✎ **EXERCISE 3 REVIEW**   Write C in front of each sentence in which all words are used correctly.

1. _____ In retrospect, she realized how many wrong decisions she had made.
2. _____ Not until the water recedes will there be good shell collecting along the beach.
3. _____ We found that the problem was insuperable and could easily be solved with a little effort.
4. _____ The kindergarten children were learning to read by the phonics method.
5. _____ He received his pedigree at the spring convocation.
6. _____ The enemy projectile just missed the city.
7. _____ It seemed like an auspicious time to present the new bill to the voters.
8. _____ We are looking for a specious house, one with at least ten rooms.
9. _____ The director tried to influence the board members, but they were recalcitrant.
10. _____ He ascribed his success to hard work and a bit of luck.
11. _____ The candidate was assiduous in canvassing every house in the district.
12. _____ The bride cast a supercilious glance at the guest who arrived in combat boots and a trench coat.
13. _____ The police were on a tour of introspection in the neighborhood.
14. _____ The doctor proscribed an antibiotic, but the child refused to swallow it.
15. _____ She was moved to tears by the pathos in the story.
16. _____ After Jack remissed on his second appointment, we realized he didn't want the job.
17. _____ He was attempting to influence his distant son through telepathy.
18. _____ The old manuscript had been copied and illustrated by scribes.
19. _____ The play ended with a prologue by the hero.
20. _____ All my arguments can be subsumed under one main argument.
21. _____ They had their property assessed for tax purposes.
22. _____ People who are superstitious also often believe in magic.
23. _____ They walked over to the syndrome to watch the football practice.
24. _____ The microwave oven has now superseded the conventional oven.
25. _____ A few of the late author's unpublished poems have been found and are now being published posthumously.
26. _____ The flood subsided before too much damage was done.
27. _____ Fidelity leads to harmonious polygamy.
28. _____ Formal logic is subject to syllogistic reasoning.
29. _____ Black and white are the only colors in the spectrum.
30. _____ Postimpressionist painters came from Africa.

TORT—to twist

If you are driving along a little-traveled mountain road, you will certainly understand the meaning of **tortuous**. It comes from the root TORT *to twist* and means full of *twists* and turns. You can speak of a tortuous road, a tortuous path through the woods, a tortuous climb down a mountain, a tortuous career with advances and reverses all along the way, or tortuous arguments that wander all over rather than moving directly toward a goal. Tortuous may also mean morally *twisted*, deceitful, not straightforward. Tortuous explanations may *twist* the truth, and tortuous deals may be *twisted* or crooked.

Tortuous must not be confused with **torturous**, which is related to torture and means inflicting physical or mental pain.

contortionist (kun tawr´ shun ist) [CON together + TORT to twist]—an acrobat who can twist the body and limbs into extraordinary positions. *At the circus, we watched an expert contortionist.*

distort (dis tawrt´) [DIS away + TORT to twist]—*lit.* to twist away; to twist from the true meaning, as to distort the facts. *Her description of the accident distorted the facts.*

extort (ik stawrt´) [EX out + TORT to twist]—*lit.* to twist something out; to obtain by violence or threat. *They tried to extort money by blackmail.*

retort (ri tawrt´) [RE back + TORT to twist]—*lit.* a twisting back on the giver; a reply to an insult or a criticism. *His retort to her criticism was shattering.*

torch (tawrch)—a portable light produced by a flammable material twisted around the end of a stick and ignited (early torches were made of twisted flax dipped in tallow). *We watched the torchlight parade.*

torment (tawr ment´)—*lit.* to twist; to annoy. *Along the shore, the mosquitoes tormented us.*

tort (tawrt)—*lit.* a twisted action; a wrongful act, injury, or damage for which a civil suit can be brought for damages. *If a person breaks a shop window, that person has committed a tort against the shop owner.*

tortoise (tawr´ tus)—a turtle, especially a land turtle, so called perhaps because of its twisted feet. *The waitress worked at the speed of a tortoise.*

tortuous (tawrch´ uh wus)—full of twists and turns. *Drive cautiously because that's a tortuous road.* Also, not straightforward; deceitful. *Her tortuous dealings gave her the reputation of being untrustworthy.*

torture (tawr´ chur)—any severe physical or mental pain. *Waiting for the judges' decision after the contest was torture.*

torturous (tawrch´ uh rus)—inflicting physical or mental pain. *The defendant had to undergo torturous questioning.*

ALSO: contortion, torque, torsion

✎ EXERCISE 1   Write the appropriate TORT word.

1. The mobster tried to _____ money in exchange for "protection."
2. The defense attorney's _____ to the prosecutor convinced the jury of his client's innocence.
3. The audience was amazed at the acrobatic performance of the _____.
4. Emphasizing unimportant details, the student tried to _____ the fact that she plagiarized her term paper.
5. Hydroplaning while driving can be _____ with the twists and turns of skidding on the wet road.
6. Having all her wisdom teeth pulled was _____.
7. The civil suit regarding that _____ was settled out of court.

✎ EXERCISE 2 REVIEW   Write C in front of each sentence in which all words are used correctly.

1. _____ The posterior legs of an animal are its front legs.
2. _____ The Preamble to the Constitution begins with the words "We the people of the United States, in order to form a more perfect Union . . . ."
3. _____ The small nation refused to be subjugated by its powerful neighbor.
4. _____ Although she did not appear ill, her friends knew she was suffering from an insidious disease.
5. _____ By a clever subterfuge, he avoided taking part in the debate.
6. _____ Her proclivity toward revealing trade secrets cost Sami her job.
7. _____ The subpoena released him from jail.
8. _____ The speaker claimed that the tax reform would be a panacea for all the ills of the country.
9. _____ She was malignant when she heard that she had been fired.
10. _____ Always a sedate person, she kicked off her shoes and sat down on the floor.
11. _____ The apathy of the committee precluded their accomplishing much.
12. _____ Preeminent in her field, she was also knowledgeable in several others.
13. _____ Most of the work in that company is done not in the main office but in the subsidiary offices.
14. _____ Everyone commiserated with him when he lost the match.
15. _____ We were amazed at her perfidious actions toward a company that had treated her well through the years.
16. _____ The department of meteorology is predicting an early spring.

TRI—three

Like UNI (one) and BI (two), TRI is easy to spot at the beginning of many words, but knowing the roots that follow often gives the words new meaning. And sometimes a TRI word has a long history. For example, **tribe** originally referred to one of the *three* groups into which the Roman people were divided.

triangle (tri´ ang gul)—a plane figure having three sides and three angles. *I learned about triangles in my geometry course.*

tribe (trīb)—originally, one of the three groups into which the Romans were divided; now, a group of people united by the same race and customs. *We bought some blankets from the Navajo tribe.*

trident (trīd´ unt) [TRI three + DENT tooth]—a long three-pronged (toothed) spear. *Neptune, the Roman god of the sea, is usually pictured holding a trident.*

triennial (tri en´ ē ul) [TRI three + ENN year]—occurring every three years. *The society held a triennial convention.*

trilateral (tri lat´ ur ul) [TRI three + LATER side]—having three sides. *The three countries signed a trilateral treaty.*

trilingual (tri ling´ gwul) [TRI three + LINGU language]—speaking three languages. *In Switzerland, many people are trilingual, speaking German, French, and Italian.*

trilogy (tril´ uh je)—three literary, dramatic, or musical compositions that, though each is complete in itself, form a related series. *Last year I read all three books of Tolkien's trilogy* The Lord of the Rings.

trinity (trin´ uh tē)—a set of three persons or things that form a unit, as the three divine persons of Christian theology. *The Apostles' Creed affirms the speaker's belief in the Trinity.*

trio (trē´ o)—any three people or things joined or associated. *The men's trio sang a concluding number.*

tripartite (tri pahr´ tīt)—composed of three parts; shared by three parties. *The three countries made a tripartite agreement.*

(Trilateral and tripartite are close synonyms.)

triplets (trip´ luts)—three children born at one birth. *The birth of triplets was a great surprise to the family.*

triplicate (trip´ li kut) [TRI three + PLIC to fold]—threefold; one of three identical copies or things. *The boss asked for the letters in triplicate.*

tripod (tri´ pahd) [TRI three + POD foot]—a three-legged stand for supporting a camera or other instrument. *Our telescope stood on a tripod.*

trivet (triv´ it)—a three-legged stand for holding a vessel or dish. *The hot dish sat on a small black trivet on a side table.*

ALSO: trigonometry, trinomial, trivia, trivial

✎ EXERCISE 1   Which TRI word names the following?

1. the three divine persons of Christian theology _____
2. a three-legged stand for hold a vessel or dish _____
3. a long, three-pronged spear _____
4. three literary compositions in a series _____

Which TRI word describes the following?

5. speaking three languages _____
6. held every three years _____
7. shared by three countries _____
8. a plane figure having three sides and three angles _____

✎ EXERCISE 2 REVIEW   Write C in front of each sentence in which all words are used correctly.

1. _____ Punctuating a sentence incorrectly can distort its meaning.
2. _____ Her kitchen contained a full panoply of modern equipment.
3. _____ The speaker was smartly dressed in a nondescript outfit.
4. _____ His unpleasant retort may precipitate a quarrel.
5. _____ Her path to fame had been tortuous, with many wins and many losses.
6. _____ Living like a recluse, he enjoyed chatting with his neighbors.
7. _____ We had fun wandering through that subterranean cave.
8. _____ The captors tried to extort a confession from their captive.
9. _____ Despite his protuberant belly, he still munches chocolate bars.
10. _____ It was a long, torturous road down the mountain.
11. _____ Anyone with a sedentary job is sure to get plenty of exercise.
12. _____ Telemetry has enabled us to discover many facts about Mars.
13. _____ The doctor was unusually perspicacious in diagnosing the illness.
14. _____ The child was precocious but had a profusion of emotional problems.
15. _____ The ads flashing on the screen for seconds had a subliminal effect on the viewers.
16. _____ Their report was a synthesis of the ideas that had been presented at the symposium.
17. _____ The director was given profuse praise by the grateful cast.
18. _____ Preponderant in my mind was the necessity of saving that forest from the developers.

VER—true

If you doubt someone's **veracity**, you doubt that person's *truthfulness*. If you speak of a **veritable** downpour of rain, you mean that it was *truly* a downpour. To **verify** something is to prove that it is *true*. When jury members give a **verdict** [VER true + DICT to speak], they are literally speaking the *truth*. Even the little word **very** comes from VER and means *truly*.

veracious (vuh ra´ shus)—truthful; accurate. *The newspaper gave a veracious account of the incident.*
veracity (vuh ras´ uh tē)—truthfulness. *No one doubted her veracity.*
verdict (vur´ dikt) [VER true + DICT to speak]—*lit.* a speaking of the truth; the decision of a jury. *The jury gave its verdict of not guilty.*
verifiable (ver´ uh fī uh bul)—capable of being proved true. *None of his statements were verifiable.*
verification (ver ruh fuh ka´ shun)—establishment of the truth. *Before cashing the check, the clerk asked for verification of the customer's identity.*
verify (ver´ u fī)—to prove something is true. *I can verify all the figures in my account.*
verily (ver´ uh lē)—an archaic word meaning truly. *"Verily, I say unto you"* is a common expression in the Bible.
veritable (ver´ uh tuh bul)—true; actual. *He was a veritable Good Samaritan.*
verity (ver´ uh tē)—a statement, principle, or belief that is considered to be established truth, as religious verities. *Alone on the mountain, he had time to ponder the external verities.*
very (ver´ ē)—truly, absolutely. *Limit your use of* very *in your compositions. The restaurant is in the very heart of the city.*

ALSO: aver, verisimilitude

✎ EXERCISE 1   Write the appropriate VER word.

1. With her amazing knowledge of facts, she's a _____ encyclopedia.

2. He'd never lie to you; you can depend on his _____.

3. I was careful to _____ each fact before presenting it.

4. The travel agent asked for _____ of the child's age.

5. You can count on her to give a _____ report of the trial because she always tells the truth.

6. Little _____ evidence could be obtained about the accident because there had been no witnesses.

7. He was now questioning some of the _____ he had always accepted in his youth.

8. The formal old way to say truly, _____, is not used in our language today.

9. Jurors must reach a unanimous _____ in murder trials.

10. We overuse the word _____.

136

✎ EXERCISE 2 REVIEW   Underline the appropriate word.

1. Their (assiduous, insidious) tactics misled their clients.
2. My sister has a (phobic, endemic) dread of air travel.
3. The dean suspected that there were (subversive, subsistence) activities going on in the dorms.
4. Because of his (xenophobia, photophobia), he had to avoid strong sunlight.
5. The police (proscribed, ascribed) the accident to drunken driving.
6. The (veracity, verdict) of the witness was never questioned.
7. The clear skies (preclude, presage) a pleasant day.
8. The contestant was (assessed, obsessed) with a desire to succeed.
9. Because I liked the first volume, I wanted to read the rest of the (trilogy, trinity).
10. The casserole sat on a small (trident, trivet) on the dining room table.
11. One group has a yearly meeting, and the other has a (triennial, trilateral) meeting.
12. The view from the (promontory, proclivity) was inspiring.
13. The Hebrews practiced (monotheism, pantheism).
14. Pencils are made from (graphite, graffiti).
15. The three countries signed a (tripartite, triennial) arms agreement.
16. The (extortionist, contortionist) blackmailed the victim for money.
17. Our Supreme Court (proscribes, transcribes) our harmful laws.
18. The importance of using (syllogisms, synopsizes) in formal logic is paramount.
19. The essay used (superfluous, supercilious) examples to support the thesis.
20. The best way to understand one's self is to become (introspective, despicable).

✎ EXERCISE 3 JOURNAL   Write several sentences in your *vocabulary journal* using words from the roots TRI and VER. Pick words you had trouble remembering.

VERT, VERS—to turn

A **verse** or line of poetry comes from the root VERS *to turn*. Just as a plow makes a furrow and then at the end of the furrow *turns* to make another parallel one, so a verse of poetry *turns* when it comes to the end of the line and goes back to make another line.

Universe also comes from the root VERS. It is made up of UNI *one* and VERS *to turn* and means literally all things that exist *turned* into one. The ancients thought all the heavenly bodies were *turning* around the Earth, *turning* into one whole.

adversary (ad´ vur ser ē) [AD against + VERS to turn]—*lit.* one turned against another; opponent. *She easily defeated her adversary in the contest.*

adverse (ad vurs´) [AD against + VERS to turn]—turned against; unfavorable. *The company had to cope with adverse publicity.*

adversity (ad vur´ suh tē) [AD against + VERS to turn]—the state of being turned against; misfortune. *His years of adversity made him sympathetic to others in trouble.*

advertise (ad vur tīz´) [AD to + VERT to turn]—to turn attention to. *I'm going to advertise my bike for sale.*

averse (uh vurs´) [AB from + VERS to turn]—*lit.* to turn from; having a feeling of great distaste. *Having lost so much money on the lottery, she was averse to risking any more.*

aversion (uh vur´ zhun) [AB away + VERS to turn]—*lit.* a turning away; extreme dislike. *Because of her aversion to work, she never held a job long.*

avert (uh vurt´) [AB away + VERT to turn]—to turn away. *She averted her eyes from the unpleasant scene.* Also, to prevent. *By taking preventive measures, they hope to avert another disaster.*

controversy (kahn´ truh vur sē) [CONTRA against + VERS to turn]—*lit.* opinions turned against each other; a dispute. *The controversy over the use of the land remained unsettled.*

convert (kun vurt´) [CON together + VERT to turn]—*lit.* to turn together to the same belief; to turn from one belief to another. *They tried to convert me to their political beliefs.*

divert (duh vurt´) [DI away + VERT to turn]—to turn away, as to turn someone's attention away from something. *I tried to listen to the lecture, but the whispering behind me diverted my attention.*

inadvertent (in ud vur´ tunt) [IN not + AD to + VERT to turn]—*lit.* not turning one's mind to a matter; unintentional. *He made an inadvertent reference to the plans for the surprise party.*

introvert (in´ truh vurt) [INTRO within + VERT to turn]—*lit.* one who turns within; one whose thoughts and interests are directed inward. *Introverts think mainly about themselves.*

obverse (ob vurs´) [OB toward + VERS to turn]—turned toward the observer; the side bearing the main design (as opposed to reverse). *The obverse side of a U.S. coin bears the main design and the date.*

perverse (pur vurs´) [PER (intensive) + VERS to turn]—turned away from what is right or good; obstinately disobedient or difficult. *Always perverse, he opposed the wishes of the group.*

universe (yoo´ nuh vurs) [UNI one + VERS to turn]—*lit.* all things that exist turned into one; everything in the heavens turned into one whole. *I'm learning about the universe in my astronomy course.*

versatile (vur´ suh tul)—able to turn easily from one subject or occupation to another; competent in many fields. *An unusually versatile actor, he is able to play any role from hero to clown.*

138

verse (vurs) [VERS to turn]—*lit.* turning from one line to the next in poetry, like a plow turning to make parallel furrows. *I wrote a verse for my Christmas cards this year.*

version (vur' zhun) [VERS to turn]—a translation or turning of one language into another, as a version of Homer; an account related from a specific point of view, as a version of an accident. *My brother's version of the accident and mine differed.*

vertebra (vur' tuh bruh)—a bone of the spinal column that turns. *A vertebra is one of 20 short, thick bones through which the spinal cord runs.*

ALSO: anniversary, converse, conversion, convertible, diverse, diversify, diversion, divorce, extrovert, incontrovertible, inverse, invertebrate, revert, subversive, versus (vs.), vertigo

EXERCISE 1   **Write the appropriate VERT, VERS word.**

1. I'd rather have him as a partner than as a(n) _____ in the game.

2. Instead of saying, "Heads or tails?" he always said, "_____ or reverse?"

3. I regretted having made a(n) _____ reference to her previous job.

4. Spending much time analyzing his thoughts, he was a true _____.

5. Completely disillusioned, he was _____ to giving any money to the project.

6. He faced the _____ with grace, which people admired.

7. During that year of _____, he lost his job and his home.

8. Our trip had to be postponed because of _____ weather.

9. When I glanced at her, she _____ her eyes.

10. My sister is a(n) _____ person, equally good at tennis, oil painting, and cooking.

11. The child molester was sent to prison for his _____ actions.

12. Many early paganists were _____ to Christianity during the Middle Ages.

13. Which _____ of the story do you prefer?

14. Shakespeare is considered one of the best writers of poetic _____.

15. At the trial, the defendant's attorney tried to _____ the jurors attention away from the facts by appealing to their emotions.

✎ **EXERCISE 2 REVIEW**   Give the meaning of each root and a word in which it is found.

ROOT	MEANING	WORD
1. METER, METR		
2. MIT, MIS, MISS		
3. MONO		
4. MORPH		
5. PAN		
6. PATH		
7. PED		
8. PHIL		
9. PHOB		
10. PHON		
11. POST		
12. PRE		
13. PRO		
14. RE		
15. SCRIB, SCRIPT		
16. SED, SID, SESS		
17. SPEC, SPIC, SPECT		
18. SUB		
19. SUPER		
20. SYN, SYM, SYL		
21. TELE		
22. TORT		
23. TRI		
24. VER		
25. VERT, VERS		

✏️ **EXERCISE 3 REVIEW**   The 12 underlined words are ones you've studied. Copy them onto the lines below and give their meanings. Understanding all the words should make rereading the paragraph satisfying.

Faced in the 1980s with the prospect of chronic oil shortages, most Americans concurred that everyone must conserve. Government edicts reduced speed limits and controlled temperatures in public buildings. Individuals overcame their propensity to drive their cars to work and no longer regarded public transportation with aversion. Others experimented with a spectrum of solutions from windmills to solar power. All the efforts taken together, though not a panacea for our energy problems, were an important prologue to what we must do to make sure some oil supplies will be left for posterity. And still today, we are struggling to find ways to circumvent the unprecedented oil shortage that threatens us.

WORD	MEANING
1. _____	_____
2. _____	_____
3. _____	_____
4. _____	_____
5. _____	_____
6. _____	_____
7. _____	_____
8. _____	_____
9. _____	_____
10. _____	_____
11. _____	_____
12. _____	_____

VIA—way

In Roman times, a place where three roads met was called the three-*way* place, or trivia (TRI three + VIA way). When people on their way to market gathered at that place to chat about unimportant matters, their talk came to be called **trivia**, or three-*way* talk. Eventually any talk about unimportant things was called **trivial**. So today, when we talk about trivial things, we are reminded of those Romans who did likewise.

deviate (de′ ve āt) [DE from + VIA way]—to turn away from an established way. *Anyone who deviates from the rules is likely to be in trouble.*

deviation (de ve ā′ shun) [DE from + VIA way]—a turning aside from an established way. *The chairperson would not tolerate the slightest deviation from parliamentary rules.*

devious (de′ ve us) [DE from + VIA way]—straying from the proper way; crooked. *His fortune had been made by devious means.*

impervious (im pur′ ve us) [IN not + PER through + VIA way]—*lit.* no way through; incapable of being passed through. *The cloth was impervious to water. His mind was impervious to reason.*

obviate (ob′ ve āt) [OB against + VIA way]—*lit.* to come against something in the way and dispose of it; to prevent. *Careful planning will obviate future difficulties.*

obvious (ob′ ve us) [OB against + VIA way]—*lit.* standing against one in the way; clearly visible; evident. *What we should do was obvious.*

previous (pre′ ve us) [PRE before + VIA way]—underway beforehand. *I learned that in a previous assignment.*

trivia (triv′ e uh) [TRI three + VIA way]—*lit.* three-way talk; originally, the commonplace matters discussed when neighborhood gossips met at the crossroads; any unimportant matters. *A knowledge of trivia is important for quiz show contestants.*

trivial (triv′ e ul) [TRI three + VIA way]—unimportant. *She became upset over the most trivial things.*

via (vi′ uh) [VIA way]—by way of. *We are going via Chicago.*

viaduct (vi′ uh dukt) [VIA way + DUC to lead]—a bridge leading a road (way) over a valley. *The viaduct takes the road over the railroad tracks.*

✎ EXERCISE 1   Write the appropriate VIA word.

1. The Romans built the first bridges, called _____.

2. Plastic is a(n) _____ material.

3. Eating well may _____ the risk of heart disease.

4. Moral corruption leads to _____ behavior.

5. Some of my friends know lots of _____ and so can speak on almost any topic.

6. Some of us avoid making decisions by _____ their importance.

✎ **EXERCISE 2 REVIEW**   Write C in front of each sentence in which all words
are used correctly. Then, in each remaining blank, write the word that should have been
used.

1. _____ A rabbit chasing a dog would be preposterous.
2. _____ I have a predilection for anything red and always try to avoid that color.
3. _____ Morpheus was so called because he was the god of the forms that sleepers see in their dreams.
4. _____ The coin collector turned the coin over to look at the obverse side.
5. _____ To get her driver's license, she had to give verification of her age.
6. _____ A true introvert, he went out of his way to make friends.
7. _____ I wasn't thinking when I made that inadvertent remark.
8. _____ Always a versatile person, she could fit into any of several jobs.
9. _____ Having been a poor baseball player himself, he felt empathy for his son,
who was having no luck in catching the ball.
10. _____ The apathetic work of everyone in the administration to further the new
plan really paid off.
11. _____ A pedigree means literally the foot of a crane because the three-line diagram
used to indicate descent looks like the foot of a crane.
12. _____ To most people, it's cacophony, but I really enjoy the sounds of an orchestra
tuning up.
13. _____ She had learned to reason according to the classic syllogisms.
14. _____ If you follow the rules, you'll obviate further trouble.
15. _____ Her perverse attitude made her a favorite in the office.
16. _____ His working full-time may be an impediment to his success in college.
17. _____ As they chatted about trivia during the musical, they were impervious to
the glances of those around them.
18. _____ As soon as the winner was announced, there was pandemonium in the
stands.
19. _____ Any deviation in following the recipe may mean failure.
20. _____ A subservient employee is usually afraid to deviate from the norm.
21. _____ Walking home from the subway, we were caught in a veritable downpour.
22. _____ You may depend upon her to give a veracious account of the proceedings.
23. _____ The officer at the border asked for veracity of my citizenship.
24. _____ She tried to divert the attention of her guests from her mischievous child.
25. _____ My friends refused to speculate on the outcome of the election.

VOC, VOKE—to call, voice

A **convocation** [CON together + VOC to call] is a *calling* together, an assembly. It may begin with an **invocation** [IN in + VOC to call], a *calling* for divine aid; and if the convocation is a college graduation, then the graduates will be looking forward to their **vocations**, or *callings*. Later, after they are settled in their jobs, they will no doubt be thinking of **avocations**, or *callings* away from their jobs.

advocate (ad´ vu kut) [AD to + VOC to call]—*lit.* one called to give evidence; a person who pleads on another's behalf or for a cause. *He was an advocate of free elections in his country.*

avocation (av u kā´ shun) [AB away + VOC to call]—*lit.* a calling away; a diversion; a hobby. *I spend almost as much time on my avocation as on my vocation.*

convocation (kahn vu kā´ shun) [CON together + VOC to call]—*lit.* a calling together; an assembly. *I hope to get my degree at the spring convocation.*

evocative (i vok´ uh tiv) [E out + VOC to call]—*lit.* calling out; calling forth. *The sounds of the forest were evocative of his early camping days.*

evoke (i vōk´) [E out + VOC to call]—*lit.* to call out; to call forth, as memories or feelings. *The smell of burning leaves always evoked memories of his childhood.*

invocation (in vuh kā´ shun) [IN in + VOC to call]—*lit.* a calling for divine aid; an opening prayer. *The invocation was given by the dean.*

invoke (in vōk´) [IN in + VOC to call]—*lit.* to call in; to call upon for aid or support. *The accused person invoked the Fifth Amendment.*

irrevocable (i rev´ uh ku bul) [IN not + RE back + VOC to call]—not capable of being called back; unalterable. *His decision was irrevocable.*

provocation (prahv uh kā´ shun) [PRO forth + VOC to call]—something that calls forth irritation. *That child cries at the slightest provocation.*

provoke (pruh vōk´) [PRO forth + VOC to call]—to call forth; to bring about; to cause anger or irritation. *His constant complaining provokes me.*

revoke (ri vōk´) [RE back + VOC to call]—to call back. *The company revoked its earlier offer.*

vocabulary (vō kab´ yuh ler ē)—*lit.* the words one can speak (call). *A large vocabulary is an asset in college.*

vocation (vo kā´ shun)—a calling; an occupation or profession. *Are you pleased with your choice of vocation?*

vociferous (vō sif´ ur us) [VOC voice + FER to carry]—*lit.* carrying a loud voice; noisy. *The crowd at the rally made a vociferous protest against the location of the nuclear power plant.*

ALSO: advocacy, equivocal, equivocate, provocative, vocal

EXERCISE 1 JOURNAL   In your *vocabulary journal,* write four sentences using VOC, VOKE words. Pick words that you have trouble remembering.

✎ **EXERCISE 2**   Write the appropriate VOC, VOKE word.

1. The chasm between the adversaries was _____.

2. Edna St. Vincent Millay's sonnets of love _____ strong pathos in the reader.

3. Religious leaders _____ God's blessings for their congregants.

4. Although he liked his vocation, his _____ of guitar playing really satisfied him.

5. When the strikers marched in front of their building, they were _____ yet civil.

6. Going back to his hometown was always a(n) _____ experience.

7. Congress always begins its session with a(n) _____.

8. Awards were presented at the spring _____.

9. His license was _____ after his third conviction for DUI.

10. Marita found her _____ in teaching.

✎ **EXERCISE 3 REVIEW**   Write C in front of each sentence in which all words are used correctly. Then, in the remaining blanks, write the word that should have been used.

1. _____ I'm not averse to helping you with your plan.

2. _____ Instead of going straight home, they took a circuitous route.

3. _____ The two countries made a trilateral agreement on arms limitation.

4. _____ We were fascinated as we watched the metamorphosis of the pupa into a moth.

5. _____ In the botany lab, we dissected a flower and named all its parts.

6. _____ We felt that the assessor gave too low an evaluation of our house.

7. _____ Adverse road conditions made our trip unpleasant.

8. _____ The superpower tried to subjugate the natives on the island.

9. _____ The secretary's proclivity toward wasting time led to her dismissal.

10. _____ The benevolence of the lodge members aided him in his time of adversity.

11. _____ If he were more versatile, he wouldn't be limited to just one kind of job.

12. _____ Suffering from claustrophobia, she refused to go to the top of the tower.

COMPREHENSIVE TEST A

Here are all 56 roots that you have learned. Give the meaning of each root and a word in which it is found.

ROOT	MEANING	WORD
1. A, AN		
2. AMBI, AMPHI		
3. ANN, ENN		
4. ANTE, ANTI		
5. ANTHROP		
6. ANTI		
7. AUTO		
8. BENE		
9. BI		
10. BIO		
11. CEDE		
12. CHRON		
13. CIRCUM		
14. COM, CON, COL, COR		
15. CRED		
16. CUR		
17. DICT		
18. DIS, DI, DIF		
19. EQU		
20. EU		
21. EX, ES, E		
22. FID		
23. GEN		
24. GRAPH, GRAM		
25. HYPER		
26. LOG		
27. -LOGY		

ROOT	MEANING	WORD
28. LOQU, LOC	_____	_____
29. MAL	_____	_____
30. METER, METR	_____	_____
31. MIT, MIS, MISS	_____	_____
32. MONO	_____	_____
33. MORPH	_____	_____
34. PAN	_____	_____
35. PATH	_____	_____
36. PED	_____	_____
37. PHIL	_____	_____
38. PHOB	_____	_____
39. PHON	_____	_____
40. POST	_____	_____
41. PRE	_____	_____
42. PRO	_____	_____
43. RE	_____	_____
44. SCRIB, SCRIPT	_____	_____
45. SED, SID, SESS	_____	_____
46. SPEC, SPIC, SPECT	_____	_____
47. SUB	_____	_____
48. SUPER	_____	_____
49. SYN, SYM, SYL	_____	_____
50. TELE	_____	_____
51. TORT	_____	_____
52. TRI	_____	_____
53. VER	_____	_____
54. VERT, VERS	_____	_____
55. VIA	_____	_____
56. VOC, VOKE	_____	_____

COMPREHENSIVE TEST B

The words in this test are taken from the words you have learned throughout the book. Your score on this test will indicate how much the study of word roots has increased your vocabulary.

1. _____ ambivalence **A.** lack of feeling **B.** conflicting feelings **C.** jealousy **D.** dislike

2. _____ misanthropic **A.** doubting **B.** hating marriage **C.** hating people **D.** generous

3. _____ antithesis **A.** secondary theme of an essay **B.** failure **C.** climax **D.** exact opposite

4. _____ automaton **A.** self-government **B.** government by a single person **C.** one who acts mechanically **D.** car buff

5. _____ beneficiary **A.** lawyer who handles wills **B.** one who receives benefits **C.** one who gives money to benefit others **D.** one who leaves money in a will

6. _____ synchronize **A.** to keep a time record **B.** to compose an accompaniment **C.** to cause to keep time together **D.** to prophesy

7. _____ circumspect **A.** cautious **B.** hardworking **C.** knowledgeable **D.** showing respect

8. _____ compunction **A.** connecting word **B.** compulsion **C.** satisfaction about something one has done **D.** a slight regret

9. _____ incredulous **A.** not believe readily **B.** believing too readily **C.** lacking credit **D.** not trustworthy

10. _____ cursory **A.** using profanity **B.** critical **C.** hateful **D.** hasty and superficial

11. _____ demagogue **A.** ancient tribal god **B.** half man and half god **C.** leader who appeals to the emotions to gain power **D.** leader who works for the good of the people

12. _____ euphonious **A.** having a pleasant sound **B.** coming from a distance **C.** false **D.** difficult to hear

13. _____ exonerate **A.** to honor **B.** to take out objectionable parts **C.** to free from blame **D.** to find guilty

14. _____ eulogy **A.** speech by an actor alone on the stage **B.** explanation of a literary passage **C.** speech blaming someone **D.** speech praising someone

15. _____ colloquial **A.** incorrect **B.** talkative **C.** conversational **D.** standard

16. _____ malevolent **A.** kindly **B.** violent **C.** giving money to others **D.** wishing evil toward others

17. _____ emissary **A.** traveler **B.** spy **C.** servant **D.** someone sent out

18. _____ anthropomorphic **A.** relating to the early Stone Age **B.** having human characteristics **C.** having animal form **D.** changing form

19. _____ panoply **A.** impressive display **B.** high covering **C.** harsh criticism **D.** series of games

20. _____ apathetic **A.** sad **B.** deserving sympathy **C.** pitiful **D.** indifferent

21. _____ expedite **A.** to experiment with **B.** to send away **C.** to speed the progress of **D.** to make clear

22. _____ propensity **A.** dislike **B.** thoughtfulness **C.** belief **D.** natural inclination

23. _____ **sedentary** **A.** temporary **B.** permanent **C.** requiring much sitting **D.** producing sediment

24. _____ **specious** **A.** having many rooms **B.** seemingly good but actually not so **C.** reasonable **D.** category of living things

25. _____ **subterfuge** **A.** deceptive strategy **B.** underwater vessel **C.** play acting **D.** hatred

26. _____ **insuperable** **A.** extraordinary **B.** easily overcome **C.** incapable of being overcome **D.** best of its kind

27. _____ **symbiosis** **A.** similarity in biologic function **B.** similarity in evolutionary development **C.** living together in close relationship **D.** use of symbols in literature

28. _____ **bicameral** **A.** two marriages **B.** two branches of government **C.** two sides **D.** two teams

29. _____ **philatelist** **A.** a stamp collector **B.** a tropical climbing plant **C.** one who loves books **D.** one who loves people

30. _____ **predilection** **A.** outweighing; having more power or importance **B.** judgment formed beforehand **C.** a preference or strong like for something **D.** outweighing, more important

31. _____ **synergy** **A.** the way words are arranged **B.** a brief general summary **C.** working together **D.** type of illness

32. _____ **obviate** **A.** to turn away from an established way **B.** no way through **C.** to prevent **D.** evident

33. _____ **vociferous** **A.** loud, noisy voice **B.** to call back **C.** talkative **D.** unalterable

34. _____ **averse** **A.** to turn away from **B.** to turn inside **C.** to turn from **D.** against, unfavorable

35. _____ **tortuous** **A.** inflicting physical or mental pain **B.** to twist or annoy **C.** full of twists and turns **D.** twisted action

COMPREHENSIVE TEST C

These words contain all the roots you have studied. Give the meaning of each root and the meaning of the word.

WORD	ROOT	MEANING OF ROOT	MEANING OF WORD
1. amphibian	AMPHI	_____	
	BIO	_____	_____
2. antedate	ANTE	_____	_____
3. anthropomorphic	ANTHROP	_____	
	MORPH	_____	_____
4. antibiotic	ANTI	_____	
	BIO	_____	_____
5. asymmetric	A	_____	
	SYM	_____	
	METR	_____	_____
6. autograph	AUTO	_____	
	GRAPH	_____	_____
7. benediction	BENE	_____	
	DICT	_____	_____
8. biennial	BI	_____	
	ENN	_____	_____
9. chronometer	CHRON	_____	
	METER	_____	_____
10. circumscribe	CIRCUM	_____	
	SCRIB	_____	_____
11. colloquial	COL	_____	
	LOQU	_____	_____
12. convert	CON	_____	
	VERT	_____	_____
13. credible	CRED	_____	_____
14. emissary	E	_____	
	MISS	_____	_____
15. equate	EQU	_____	_____
16. euphony	EU	_____	
	PHON	_____	_____
17. evoke	E	_____	
	VOC	_____	_____

WORD	ROOT	MEANING OF ROOT	MEANING OF WORD
18. expedient	EX	_____	
	PED	_____	_____
19. fidelity	FID	_____	_____
20. genealogy	GEN	_____	
	-LOGY	_____	_____
21. malady	MAL	_____	_____
22. monogram	MONO	_____	
	GRAM	_____	_____
23. pandemic	PAN	_____	
	DEM	_____	_____
24. philanthropy	PHIL	_____	
	ANTHROP	_____	_____
25. phobia	PHOB	_____	_____
26. prologue	PRO	_____	
	LOG	_____	_____
27. prospectus	PRO	_____	
	SPECT	_____	_____
28. retort	RE	_____	
	TORT	_____	_____
29. subside	SUB	_____	
	SID	_____	_____
30. superannuated	SUPER	_____	
	ANN	_____	_____
31. telepathy	TELE	_____	
	PATH	_____	_____
32. trivia	TRI	_____	
	VIA	_____	_____
33. verify	VER	_____	_____
34. amorphous	A	_____	
	MORPH	_____	_____
35. intercede	CON	_____	
	CEDE	_____	_____
36. panacea	PAN	_____	_____
37. synod	SYN, SYM	_____	_____
38. hyperbole	HYPER	_____	_____
39. vociferous	VOC, VOKE	_____	_____
40. precede	PRE CEDE	_____	_____

COMPREHENSIVE TEST D

The words in these sentences contain the roots you have studied. Put a C in front of each sentence in which all words are used correctly. No answers are provided at the back of the book for this test.

1. _____ He felt apathetic about his job, not caring whether he kept it or not.

2. _____ The bald eagle, an amphibian, is the national bird of the United States.

3. _____ A triennial convention is held every three years.

4. _____ My mother plants perennials so she won't have to buy new plants each year.

5. _____ The anterior legs of an animal are those at the front.

6. _____ Gorillas and zebras are anthropoids.

7. _____ Our contestant found that he faced a powerful antagonist.

8. _____ Taking no interest in her work, she performed it like an automaton.

9. _____ The monarch had a benign attitude toward his subjects, always thinking of their welfare.

10. _____ The new highway bisects the city.

11. _____ The biopsy proved that the growth was benign.

12. _____ Her chronic cough has lasted for years.

13. _____ She takes forever to say anything because she uses so many circumlocutions.

14. _____ A coherent paper is well organized and sticks to the point.

15. _____ A four-year-old is amazingly credulous and will believe anything you say.

16. _____ Television was the precursor of movies.

17. _____ An endemic plant is one that is widespread over the entire earth.

18. _____ A jurisdiction is a sentence given by a judge to someone who is guilty.

19. _____ He was disconcerted by the noise in the back of the auditorium.

20. _____ Becoming upset over the criticism, he lost his usual equanimity.

21. _____ After I lost that tennis match, I was in a state of euphoria.

22. _____ Receiving that scholarship expedited my getting through college.

23. _____ She accused him of fidelity and threatened to get a divorce.

24. _____ He has always been diffident and dreads speaking in public.

25. _____ Praise often engenders greater loyalty in employees.

26. _____ By using many details, he gave a graphic picture of the storm.

27. _____ The play began with a monologue between the two main characters.

28. _____ Studying word roots in this book has sparked my interest in etymology.

29. _____ Her loquacious phone calls show up on my phone bill.

30. _____ I missed class because I was really ill; I wasn't malingering.

31. _____ The odometer indicated that my blood pressure was above normal.

32. _____ A missive is a weapon.

33. _____ Monogamy is the belief that there is only one God.
34. _____ The lecturer's presentation was simply an amorphous collection of unrelated stories.
35. _____ Do you expect the self-help group to be a panacea for all your problems?
36. _____ She felt extreme antipathy for her sister and liked to spend as much time with her as she could.
37. _____ Improving my vocabulary has impeded my ability to read with understanding.
38. _____ He's a born philanthropist, criticizing everyone and hating people in general.
39. _____ Because of her claustrophobia, she refused to enter the cave.
40. _____ Polyphonic means having two or more melodies combined.
41. _____ Because I want to leave a record for posterity, I'm writing our family history.
42. _____ Being given a month's vacation was unprecedented; no one had ever been given that long a vacation before.
43. _____ As a proponent of conservation, he has been making speeches advocating paper recycling.
44. _____ Now that she has established new habits, she's not likely to revert to the old ones.
45. _____ A new employee needs to be circumspect about offering suggestions.
46. _____ Abraham Lincoln ascribed his success to his mother.
47. _____ Because I have a sedentary job, I try to walk a mile every evening.
48. _____ When I was in France, I didn't find my inability to speak French an insuperable barrier.
49. _____ Symbiosis is the living together of two different organisms in what is usually a mutually beneficial relationship.
50. _____ Telepathy is the sending of messages by Morse code.
51. _____ The tortuous mountain road was nothing but twists and turns.
52. _____ He went sailing on the lake in his subterfuge.
53. _____ I'd never question her veracity because I've known her for years and have always found her truthful.
54. _____ She was excoriated for her treatment of the prisoners at Guantanomo Bay.
55. _____ "Walk with you I will" is an example of hyperbaton.

ANSWERS

PP. 8–9 PRELIMINARY TEST

1. B	**8.** A	**15.** D	**22.** C	**29.** B
2. D	**9.** B	**16.** C	**23.** D	**30.** D
3. A	**10.** C	**17.** D	**24.** B	**31.** C
4. A	**11.** D	**18.** B	**25.** C	**32.** A
5. D	**12.** A	**19.** A	**26.** A	**33.** C
6. B	**13.** A	**20.** C	**27.** D	
7. C	**14.** B	**21.** B	**28.** A	

P. 13 EXERCISE 1

1. anecdotes	**4.** atypical	**7.** agnostic	**10.** anemia
2. asymmetrical	**5.** Anarchy	**8.** amoral	**11.** anomaly
3. anonymous	**6.** atheist	**9.** anesthetic	

P. 13 EXERCISE 2

1. D	**2.** A	**3.** E	**4.** B	**5.** C

P. 15 EXERCISE 1

1. C	**3.** G	**5.** B
2. F	**4.** D	**6.** E

P. 15 EXERCISE 2

1. ambience	**4.** ambivalence	**7.** ambiguity	**10.** ambivalent
2. amphibious	**5.** amphibians	**8.** ambitious	
3. ambidextrous	**6.** amphitheater	**9.** ambiguous	

P. 17 EXERCISE 1

1. annual	**4.** superannuated	**7.** annals	**10.** annuity
2. biannual or semiannual	**5.** millennium	**8.** perennial	
3. centennial	**6.** per annum	**9.** anniversary	

P. 17 EXERCISE 2

1. biannually or semiannually	**3.** annuity	**5.** superannuated
2. biennial	**4.** Annals	

P. 17 EXERCISE 3 REVIEW

1. anomaly	**4.** amphibious	**7.** centennial	**10.** perennial
2. ambitious	**5.** anecdotes	**8.** amphibians	
3. ambivalent	**6.** anemia	**9.** anniversary	

P. 19 EXERCISE 1

1. antiquated
2. anteroom
3. antique
4. anticipated
5. ante
6. anterior
7. antiquarian
8. anticipate
9. antiquity
10. ante meridiem (A.M.)

P. 19 EXERCISE 2

1, 2, 5 are correct.

P. 21 EXERCISE 1

1. anthropomorphic
2. philanthropist
3. anthropologist
4. misanthrope
5. anthropoid
6. philanthropic
7. philanthropy
8. anthropomorphism
9. misanthropic
10. anthropology

P. 21 EXERCISE 3 REVIEW

1. A, AN	not, without	student choice	(see p. 12)
2. AMBI, AMPHI	around, both	student choice	(see p. 14)
3. ANN, ENN	year	student choice	(see p. 16)
4. ANTE, ANTI	before	student choice	(see p. 18)
5. ANTHROP	human	student choice	(see p. 20)

P. 23 EXERCISE 1

1. E
2. H
3. F
4. I
5. C
6. D
7. B
8. A
9. G

P. 23 EXERCISE 2

1. anticlimax
2. antiseptic
3. antagonist
4. Antarctica
5. antibiotics
6. antidote
7. antithesis

P. 25 EXERCISE 1

1. autopsy
2. automatic
3. autonomy
4. autonomic
5. autocratic
6. automaton
7. autonomous

P. 25 EXERCISE 2 REVIEW

The following are correct: 2, 3, 4, 6, 8, 9, 11, 13.

P. 26 EXERCISE 1

1. B   2. D   3. E   4. A   5. C

P. 27 EXERCISE 2

1. beneficial
2. beneficiary
3. benediction
4. benevolent
5. benefits
6. benevolence
7. benign
8. beneficence
9. benefactor

P. 27 EXERCISE 3 REVIEW
1. C
2. antidote
3. C
4. autonomic
5. anthropoids
6. C
7. C
8. C
9. misanthropic
10. C

P. 29 EXERCISE 1
1. bicuspid
2. bilingual
3. bicameral
4. bigamy
5. bipartisan
6. bicentennial
7. bilateral
8. bipeds
9. bisects
10. bivalve

P. 29 EXERCISE 2
1. bicameral
2. bicuspid
3. bilingual
4. bicentennial
5. bigamy

P. 31 EXERCISE 1
1. C
2. C
3. C
4. biofeedback
5. C
6. biopsy
7. C
8. C

P. 31 EXERCISE 2 REVIEW
1. symbiotic
2. philanthropic
3. C
4. biped
5. C
6. C
7. C
8. C
9. amoral
10. C
11. C
12. C
13. C
14. antiquated
15. C

P. 33 EXERCISE 1
1. recede
2. succeed
3. retrocede
4. intercede
5. exceed

P. 33 EXERCISE 3
1. precedent
2. seceded
3. recedes
4. exceeds
5. proceed

P. 34 EXERCISE 1
1. chronology
2. chronic
3. synchronize
4. chronometer
5. chronological
6. anachronism
7. Chronicles

P. 35 EXERCISE 2 REVIEW
1. chronicle
2. anarchy
3. bicameral
4. antique
5. exceed
6. anachronism
7. misanthropic
8. biofeedback
9. autonomous

P. 35 EXERCISE 3 REVIEW

1. A, AN	not, without	student choice	(see p. 12)
2. AMBI, AMPHI	around, both	student choice	(see p. 14)
3. ANN, ENN	year	student choice	(see p. 16)
4. ANTE/ANTI	against, opposite	student choice	(see p. 18)
5. ANTHROP	human	student choice	(see p. 20)
6. ANTI	against, opposite	student choice	(see pp. 22–23)
7. AUTO	self	student choice	(see p. 24)
8. BENE	well, good	student choice	(see p. 26)
9. BI	two	student choice	(see p. 28)
10. BIO	life	student choice	(see p. 30)

P. 37 EXERCISE 2

1. circumlocution
2. circumnavigated
3. circumvent
4. circuit
5. circumspect
6. circuitous
7. circumstances
8. circumscribe
9. circumference

P. 37 EXERCISE 3 REVIEW

1. C
2. C
3. bisect
4. C
5. centennial
6. C
7. C
8. C
9. biosphere
10. C
11. anniversary
12. C

P. 39 EXERCISE 1

1. coherent
2. collusion
3. composition
4. consummate
5. commotion
6. convivial
7. complicated
8. collaborated
9. condone
10. contemporary

P. 40 EXERCISE 2

1. commensurate
2. condone
3. correlate
4. compunction
5. commiserate
6. consensus
7. collaborate
8. congenital
9. coherent
10. convene

P. 41 EXERCISE 4 REVIEW

1. biology
2. amphibians or bivalves
3. amphibians or bivalves
4. circuitous
5. biodegradable
6. ambivalent
7. condone
8. compunction
9. perennial

P. 43 EXERCISE 1

1. incredulous
2. incredible
3. miscreant
4. credible
5. credit
6. credentials
7. incredulity
8. credence
9. credibility
10. credulous

P. 43 EXERCISE 2

1. D
2. B
3. E
4. C
5. A
6. F

P. 43 EXERCISE 3

1. credit
2. incredulity
3. credentials
4. discredit
5. creed

P. 45 EXERCISE 1

1. C
2. E
3. A
4. F
5. B
6. D

P. 45 EXERCISE 2

1. concurrent
2. excursion
3. currency
4. current
5. curriculum
6. course
7. recurrent
8. concur
9. cursory
10. concourse

P. 47 EXERCISE 2

1. pandemic
2. epidemic
3. Demographic
4. democracy
5. endemic
6. demagogue

P. 47 EXERCISE 3 REVIEW

1. A, AN	not, without	student choice	(see p. 12)
2. AMBI, AMPHI	around, both	student choice	(see p. 14)
3. ANN, ENN	year	student choice	(see p. 16)
4. ANTE, ANTI	against, opposite	student choice	(see p. 18)
5. ANTHROP	human	student choice	(see p. 20)
6. ANTI	against, opposite	student choice	(see pp. 22–23)
7. AUTO	self	student choice	(see p. 24)
8. BENE	well, good	student choice	(see p. 26)
9. BI	two	student choice	(see p. 28)
10. BIO	life	student choice	(see p. 30)
11. CEDE, CEED	go, yield, give away	student choice	(see p. 32)
12. CHRON	time	student choice	(see p. 34)
13. CIRCUM	around	student choice	(see p. 36)
14. COM, CON, COL, COR	together, with	student choice	(see pp. 38–39)
15. CRED	to believe	student choice	(see p. 42)
16. CUR	to run	student choice	(see p. 44)

P. 49 EXERCISE 2

1. abdicated
2. dictated
3. jurisdiction
4. valedictorian
5. addict
6. diction
7. dictatorial
8. predicts
9. edict
10. dictionary
11. contradict

P. 49 EXERCISE 3 REVIEW

1. bigamy
2. anthropology
3. beneficiary
4. biped
5. amoral
6. anachronism
7. credence
8. collusion
9. circumspect
10. chronic

P. 51 EXERCISE 1

1. disarray
2. dismantle
3. disparate
4. disseminate
5. discordant
6. disparity
7. disburse
8. diverse
9. dissident
10. dissuade

P. 51 EXERCISE 2

1. C
2. B
3. F
4. D
5. A
6. E

P. 52 EXERCISE 3 REVIEW

1. biannual
2. credibility
3. ambitious
4. curriculum
5. endemic
6. discourse
7. complicate
8. chronicle
9. excursion
10. concurrent

P. 53 EXERCISE 5 REVIEW

1. asymmetrical — A — not
2. ambiguity — AMBI — both
3. autocrat — AUTO — self
4. biology — BIO — life
5. circumvent — CIRCUM — around
6. credible — CRED — to believe
7. demographic — DEM — people
8. disparity — DIS — not, away, apart
9. biannual — BI — two
10. synchronize — CHRON — time
11. collusion — COL — together, with
12. courier — CUR — to run
13. jurisdiction — DICT — speak
14. dismantle — DIS — not, away, apart
15. semiannual — ANN — year
16. anterior — ANTE — before
17. anthropology — ANTHROP — human
18. antithesis — ANTI — against, opposite
19. benign — BENE — good, well
20. bisect — BI — two
21. chronicle — CHRON — time
22. compunction — COM — together, with
23. exceed — CEED — go, yield
24. current — CUR — run
25. anomaly — AN — not, without

P. 55 EXERCISE 1

1. equate
2. equivocated
3. equity
4. equanimity
5. equilibrium
6. equable
7. equinox
8. equilateral
9. equivocal
10. equitable
11. adequate
12. equivalent
13. equator

P. 55 EXERCISE 2 REVIEW

Numbers 1, 3, 4, 5, 8, 9 are correct.

P. 56 EXERCISE 1

1. euphoria
2. euphonious
3. eulogize

4. euthanasia
5. euphemism

P. 57 EXERCISE 2

1. euthanasia
2. euphonious
3. eulogy

4. euphoria
5. eulogized
6. euphony

7. euphemisms

P. 57 EXERCISE 3 REVIEW

Numbers 2, 3, 4, 5, 6, 8, 9, 10, 11, 13, 15 are correct.

P. 59 EXERCISE 1

1. exonerate
2. expurgated
3. euphemism

4. eradicated
5. expatiated
6. excoriated

7. ebullient
8. emolument
9. excavate

10. expatriate

P. 59 EXERCISE 2

1. H
2. A

3. E
4. B

5. F
6. D

7. C
8. G

P. 60 EXERCISE 3 REVIEW

All answers are correct except 2, 10, 14, 15.

P. 61 EXERCISE 5 REVIEW

1. A, AN	not, without	student choice	(see p. 12)
2. AMBI, AMPHI	around, both	student choice	(see p. 14)
3. ANN, ENN	year	student choice	(see p. 16)
4. ANTE, ANTI	against, opposite	student choice	(see p. 18)
5. ANTHROP	human	student choice	(see p. 20)
6. ANTI	against, opposite	student choice	(see pp. 22–23)
7. AUTO	self	student choice	(see p. 24)
8. BENE	well, good	student choice	(see p. 26)
9. BI	two	student choice	(see p. 28)
10. BIO	life	student choice	(see p. 30)
11. CEDE, CEED	go, yield, give away	student choice	(see p. 32)
12. CHRON	time	student choice	(see p. 34)
13. CIRCUM	around	student choice	(see p. 36)
14. COM, CON, COL, COR	together, with	student choice	(see pp. 38–39)
15. CRED	to believe	student choice	(see p. 42)
16. CUR	to run	student choice	(see p. 44)
17. DEM	people	student choice	(see p. 46)
18. DICT	to speak	student choice	(see p. 48)
19. DIS, DI, DIF	not, away, apart	student choice	(see pp. 50–51)
20. EQU	equal	student choice	(see p. 54)
21. EU	good, well	student choice	(see p. 56)
22. EX, ES, E	out	student choice	(see pp. 58–59)

PP. 62–63 EXERCISE 1

1. bona fide
2. diffident
3. perfidious
4. infidel
5. fidelity
6. confidant
7. confide
8. confidential
9. infidelity
10. confident

P. 63 EXERCISE 2 REVIEW

1. incredulous
2. equanimity
3. consensus
4. benefactor
5. ambivalent
6. antithesis
7. concur
8. incredible

P. 63 EXERCISE 3 REVIEW

Answers will vary.

P. 65 EXERCISE 1

1. generates
2. genial
3. genetics
4. generic
5. genre
6. genesis
7. Gentlemen
8. engender
9. progeny
10. ingenious
11. genealogy
12. genocide

P. 66 EXERCISE 2

1. progenitors
2. genes
3. genial
4. Hydrogen
5. generous
6. Generation

P. 67 EXERCISE 5 REVIEW

Sentences 2, 3, 5, 8, 9, 10, 12, 13, 14, 15 are correct.

P. 69 EXERCISE 1

1. calligraphy
2. programs
3. autographs
4. holograms
5. geography
6. graffiti
7. graphic
8. choreography
9. monogram
10. seismograph
11. stenographer
12. geography
13. topography
14. epigrams
15. cardiogram

P. 71 EXERCISE 1

1. C
2. H
3. D
4. F
5. A
6. B
7. G
8. E

P. 71 EXERCISE 2

1. hypercritical
2. hyperbole
3. hyperopic
4. hypertrophy
5. hyperbaton
6. hypertension
7. hypertension
8. hyperactive

P. 72 EXERCISE 3 REVIEW

1. ingenious
2. confidant
3. emigrate
4. euphoria
5. disarray
6. edict
7. endemic
8. recurrent
9. circuit
10. biofeedback

P. 73 EXERCISE 6 REVIEW

1.	A, AN	not, without; unusual or irregular
2.	CHRON	time
3.	CRED	to believe
4.	DEM	people
5.	ANTHROP	human
6.	GRAPH, GRAM	to write
7.	GEN	birth, race, kind
8.	EX, ES, E	out
9.	BENE	good
10.	EU	good, well
11.	FID	faith
12.	ANTE, ANTI	before
13.	ANTI	against, opposite
14.	DIS, DI, DIF	not, away, apart
15.	COM, CON, COL, COR	together, with

P. 74 EXERCISE 1

1. D
2. A
3. E
4. B
5. C

P. 75 EXERCISE 2

1. apology
2. travelogue
3. dialogue
4. prologue
5. monologue
6. analogous

P. 75 EXERCISE 3 REVIEW

All are correct except for 3, 6, 7.

P. 75 EXERCISE 4 REVIEW

1. E
2. G
3. F
4. A
5. C
6. D
7. B
8. H

P. 77 EXERCISE 1

1. psychology
2. meteorology
3. etymology
4. geology
5. archeology
6. entomology
7. ornithology
8. embryology
9. ecology

P. 77 EXERCISE 2

1. entomology
2. astrology
3. embryology
4. anthropology
5. etymology

P. 78 EXERCISE 1

1. loquacious
2. colloquial
3. grandiloquent
4. soliloquy
5. ventriloquist
6. colloquium
7. eloquent

P. 79 EXERCISE 3 REVIEW

All are correct except 3, 8, 9, 12, 14.

P. 82 EXERCISE 1

1. malady
2. malcontent
3. malignant
4. maligned
5. malicious
6. malaise
7. malfeasance
8. malediction
9. malinger
10. malaria
11. malapropisms
12. maladroit
13. malevolent
14. malice

PP. 82–83 EXERCISE 2 REVIEW

All are correct except 1, 6.

P. 83 EXERCISE 3 REVIEW

1. graphic
2. democracy
3. consensus
4. ambiguous
5. engender
6. grandiloquent
7. eulogize
8. malign
9. anticlimax
10. perennial

PP. 84–85 EXERCISE 4 REVIEW

1. A, AN	not, without	student choice
2. AMBI, AMPHI	around, both	student choice
3. ANN, ENN	year	student choice
4. ANTE, ANTI	before	student choice
5. ANTHROP	human	student choice
6. ANTI	against, opposite	student choice
7. AUTO	self	student choice
8. BENE	well, good	student choice
9. BI	two	student choice
10. BIO	life	student choice
11. CEDE, CEED	yield, go, give away	student choice
12. CHRON	time	student choice
13. CIRCUM	around	student choice
14. COM, CON, COL, COR	together, with	student choice
15. CRED	to believe	student choice
16. CUR	to run	student choice
17. DEM	people	student choice
18. DICT	to speak	student choice
19. DIS, DI, DIF	not, away, apart	student choice
20. EQU	equal	student choice
21. EU	good, well	student choice
22. EX, ES, E	out	student choice
23. FID	faith	student choice
24. GEN	birth, race, kind	student choice
25. GRAPH, GRAM	to invite	student choice
26. HYPER	above	student choice
27. LOG	speech, word	student choice
28. -LOGY	study of	student choice
29. LOQU, LOC	to speak	student choice
30. MAL	bad	student choice

P. 87 EXERCISE 1

1. perimeter
2. barometer
3. odometer
4. kilometer
5. metronome
6. pedometer
7. symmetrical
8. tachometer
9. parameter
10. geometry

P. 87 EXERCISE 2 REVIEW

1. disproportionate
2. expatiated
3. cursory
4. loquacious
5. disconcerted
6. anthropoids
7. diffident
8. eradicated
9. equinox
10. disparity

PP. 88–89 EXERCISE 1

1. dismiss
2. omit
3. emissary
4. premise
5. intermittent

P. 89 EXERCISE 2 REVIEW

All sentences are correct except 2, 5, 6, 7, 12, 14, 15, 19, 20, 21.

PP. 90–91 EXERCISE 1

1. monosyllable
2. monotheism
3. monotone
4. monogamy
5. monolithic
6. monoliths
7. monarch
8. monocle
9. monks
10. monotonous
11. monastery

P. 91 EXERCISE 2 REVIEW

All are correct except 7, 10, 12.

P. 92 EXERCISE 1

1. endomorphic
2. morphology
3. Morphine
4. mesomorphic
5. amorphous
6. ectomorphic
7. metamorphosis
8. Morpheus

P. 93 EXERCISE 2 REVIEW

1. C
2. C
3. benediction
4. C
5. C
6. C
7. malevolent
8. C
9. C
10. C

P. 93 EXERCISE 3 REVIEW

1. atheist
2. philanthropist
3. anthropologist
4. dissident
5. antiquarian

P. 93 EXERCISE 4 REVIEW

1. C
2. E
3. A
4. D
5. B

PP. 94–95 EXERCISE 1

1. pandemonium
2. panacea
3. pantheism
4. panorama
5. pantomime
6. panoply
7. pantheon
8. panchromatic
9. Pan-American

P. 95 EXERCISE 2 REVIEW

1. CEDE, CEED   student choice
2. CIRCUM   student choice
3. COM, CON, COL, COR   student choice
4. CRED   student choice
5. CUR   student choice
6. DEM   student choice
7. DICT   student choice
8. DIS, DI, DIF   student choice
9. EQU   student choice
10. EU   student choice
11. EX, ES, E   student choice
12. FID   student choice
13. GEN   student choice
14. GRAPH, GRAM   student choice
15. HYPER   student choice
16. LOG   student choice
17. -LOGY   student choice
18. LOQU, LOC   student choice
19. MAL   student choice
20. METER, METR   student choice
21. MIT, MIS, MISS   student choice
22. MONO   student choice
23. MORPH   student choice
24. PAN   student choice

P. 97 EXERCISE 1

1. empathy
2. pathology
3. psychopathic
4. antipathy
5. Sympathy
6. pathos
7. apathetic
8. apathy
9. pathetic
10. pathological

P. 97 EXERCISE 2 REVIEW

1. D
2. E
3. A
4. C
5. F
6. B
7. G
8. I
9. J
10. H

PP. 98–99 EXERCISE 1

1. expedite
2. expedient
3. impede
4. pedigree
5. impediment
6. expedition
7. pedestrian
8. quadrupeds, pedal

P. 99 EXERCISE 2 REVIEW

1. equable
2. ingenious
3. ebullient
4. disparity
5. around
6. euphonious

P. 99 EXERCISE 3 REVIEW

1. census
2. demographic
3. expedite
4. apathy
5. beneficiaries

P. 101 EXERCISE 1

1. B
2. E
3. F
4. C
5. D
6. A

P. 101 EXERCISE 2 REVIEW

1. morphology
2. etymology
3. monolithic
4. calligraphy
5. malfeasance
6. antipathy
7. pantomime
8. expedite
9. perfidious
10. analogy
11. philatelist
12. pantheon
13. equitable
14. panchromatic
15. impede

P. 102 EXERCISE 1

1. photophobia
2. acrophobia
3. xenophobia
4. claustrophobia
5. hydrophobia
6. technophobia
7. phobia

P. 103 EXERCISE 2 REVIEW

1. A, AN	not, without	student choice
2. ANTHROP	human	student choice
3. ANTE, ANTI	before	student choice
4. AUTO	self	student choice
5. BENE	good	student choice
6. CEDE	yield, go, give away	student choice
7. COM, CON, COL, COR	together with	student choice
8. CUR	to run	student choice
9. DICT	to speak	student choice
10. DIS, DI, DIF	not, away, apart	student choice
11. EQU	equal	student choice
12. EU	good, well	student choice
13. EX, ES, E	out	student choice
14. FID	faith	student choice
15. GEN	birth, race, kind	student choice
16. GRAPH, GRAM	to write	student choice
17. HYPER	over, above	student choice
18. LOG	speech, word	student choice
19. -LOGY	study of	student choice
20. LOQU, LOC	to speak	student choice
21. MAL	bad	student choice
22. METER, METR	measure	student choice
23. MIT, MIS, MISS	to send	student choice
24. MONO	one	student choice
25. MORPH	to change	student choice
26. PAN	all	student choice
27. PATH	feeling, suffering	student choice
28. PED	foot	student choice
29. PHIL	to love	student choice
30. PHOB	fear	student choice

P. 104 EXERCISE 1

1. D
2. E
3. B
4. C
5. A

P. 105 EXERCISE 2

1. cacophony
2. polyphonic
3. saxophone
4. megaphone
5. phonetics

P. 105 EXERCISE 3 REVIEW

1. C
2. C
3. C
4. missiles
5. C
6. C
7. C
8. C
9. claustrophobia
10. C
11. C

P. 107 EXERCISE 2

1. posthumously
2. posterity
3. preposterous
4. posterior
5. postlude
6. Postimpressionists
7. postmortem
8. postdated
9. postgraduate
10. post meridiem
11. postpone
12. postscript

P. 107 EXERCISE 3 REVIEW

1. emolument
2. excoriate
3. disparate
4. equivocate
5. disconcerted
6. xenophobia
7. dissidents
8. monocle
9. ambience
10. biannual
11. postlude
12. odometer
13. pathology
14. hyperactive
15. Proceed

P. 109 EXERCISE 1

1. precipitated
2. precocious
3. precedent
4. predilection
5. unprecedented
6. preeminent
7. precise
8. preamble
9. prejudiced
10. prevailed
11. prerequisite
12. prelude
13. preponderant
14. presage

P. 111 EXERCISE 1

1. prospectus
2. proclivity or propensity
3. proponent
4. protuberant
5. procrastinate
6. profusion
7. promontory
8. provident
9. profuse
10. proclaimed
11. propelled, promotion

P. 111 EXERCISE 3 REVIEW

1. D
2. F
3. E.
4. A
5. C
6. B

P. 113 EXERCISE 1

1. recession
2. recalcitrant
3. revert
4. resilience
5. remission
6. recluse
7. Renaissance
8. recant
9. remiss
10. recalcitrant
11. retain
12. recreation
13. remit
14. revive
15. retain

P. 114 EXERCISE 2 REVIEW

1. C
2. C
3. C
4. monogram
5. C
6. C
7. C
8. astronomy
9. C
10. C

P. 114 EXERCISE 3 REVIEW

1. presages
2. credible
3. etymology
4. addict
5. diffident
6. discomfited
7. ebullient
8. precise

P. 115 EXERCISE 4 REVIEW

1. antedate
2. excoriated
3. euphoric
4. engendered
5. panoply
6. pandemic
7. predicts
8. propensity
9. unprecedented
10. cacophony
11. consensus
12. proceed
13. hyperactivity
14. commensurate
15. geometry

P. 117 EXERCISE 1

1. ascribe
2. nondescript
3. transcribe
4. conscription
5. subscribe
6. proscribed

P. 117 EXERCISE 2 REVIEW

All sentences are correct except 3, 8, 9, 14, 16, 17.

P. 119 EXERCISE 1

1. sedentary
2. assiduous
3. subsidy
4. insidious
5. subside
6. superseded
7. obsession
8. subsidiary
9. obsessed
10. assess
11. assessor
12. siege
13. sedative
14. presides
15. session
16. sediment

P. 121 EXERCISE 1

1. auspicious
2. perspective
3. retrospect
4. introspection
5. despicable
6. perspicacious
7. specious
8. spectrum
9. specter
10. speculate

P. 121 EXERCISE 2 REVIEW

1. C
2. A
3. B
4. E
5. D
6. F
7. G
8. I
9. H
10. J

P. 123 EXERCISE 1

1. submerged
2. subjected
3. subsistence
4. subversive
5. subterfuge
6. subservient
7. subjugate
8. subliminal
9. subsumed
10. subpoena
11. subterranean
12. sub rosa
13. submit

P. 125 EXERCISE 1

1. supersonic
2. superfluous, surplus
3. superimpose
4. insuperable
5. supercilious

P. 125 EXERCISE 2

1. superstition
2. supervise
3. superior
4. supreme
5. soprano
6. superb
7. superfluous
8. supernumerary
9. supervisor
10. surplus

P. 127 EXERCISE 1

1. synopsis
2. symposium
3. Synthetic
4. syndrome
5. synod
6. syntax
7. syllogism
8. synergistic
9. symbol
10. synagogue

P. 128 EXERCISE 2 REVIEW

1.	A, AN	not, without	student choice
2.	ANTHROP	human	student choice
3.	ANTE, ANTI	before	student choice
4.	AUTO	self	student choice
5.	BENE	good	student choice
6.	CEDE	yield, go, give away	student choice
7.	COM, CON, COL, COR	together with	student choice
8.	CUR	to run	student choice
9.	DICT	to speak	student choice
10.	DIS, DI, DIF	not, away, apart	student choice
11.	EQU	equal	student choice
12.	EU	good, well	student choice
13.	EX, ES, E	out	student choice
14.	FID	faith	student choice
15.	GEN	birth, race, kind	student choice
16.	GRAPH, GRAM	to write	student choice
17.	HYPER	over, above	student choice
18.	LOG	speech, word	student choice
19.	-LOGY	study of	student choice
20.	LOQU, LOC	to speak	student choice
21.	MAL	bad	student choice
22.	METER, METR	measure	student choice
23.	MIT, MIS, MISS	to send	student choice
24.	MONO	one	student choice
25.	MORPH	to change	student choice
26.	PAN	all	student choice
27.	PATH	feeling, suffering	student choice
28.	PED	foot	student choice
29.	PHIL	to love	student choice
30.	PHOB	fear	student choice
31.	PHON	sound	student choice
32.	POST	after	student choice
33.	PRE	before	student choice
34.	PRO	forward, before, for, forth	student choice
35.	RE	back, again	student choice

36. SCRIB, SCRIPT	to write	student choice
37. SID, SED, SESS	to sit	student choice
38. SPEC, SPIC, SPECT	to look	student choice

P. 130 EXERCISE 1

1. Telemetry

2. telescope

3. telepathy

4. television, telephone

P. 130 EXERCISE 2 REVIEW

1. D

2. E

3. A

4. B

5. C

P. 131 EXERCISE 3 REVIEW

All sentences are correct except 3, 5, 8, 13, 14, 16, 19, 23, 27, 29, 30.

P. 133 EXERCISE 1

1. extort

2. retort

3. contortionist

4. distort

5. tortuous

6. torturous

7. tort

P. 133 EXERCISE 2 REVIEW

All sentences are correct except 1, 6, 9, 10.

P. 135 EXERCISE 1

1. Trinity

2. trivet

3. trident

4. trilogy

5. trilingual

6. triennial

7. tripartite

8. triangle

P. 135 EXERCISE 2 REVIEW

All sentences are correct except 3, 6, 10, 11.

P. 136 EXERCISE 1

1. veritable

2. veracity

3. verify

4. verification

5. veracious

6. verifiable

7. verities

8. verily

9. verdict

10. very

P. 137 EXERCISE 2 REVIEW

1. insidious

2. phobic

3. subversive

4. photophobia

5. ascribed

6. veracity

7. presage

8. obsessed

9. trilogy

10. trivet

11. triennial

12. promontory

13. monotheism

14. graphite

15. tripartite

16. extortionist

17. proscribes

18. syllogisms

19. superfluous

20. introspective

P. 139 EXERCISE 1

1. adversary	**4.** introvert	**7.** adversity	**10.** versatile	**13.** version
2. obverse	**5.** averse	**8.** adverse	**11.** perverse	**14.** verse
3. inadvertent	**6.** controversy	**9.** averted	**12.** converts	**15.** divert

P. 140 EXERCISE 2 REVIEW

1. METER, METR	measure	student choice
2. MIT, MIS, MISS	to send	student choice
3. MONO	one	student choice
4. MORPH	form	student choice
5. PAN	all	student choice
6. PATH	feeling, suffering	student choice
7. PED	foot	student choice
8. PHIL	to love	student choice
9. PHOB	fear	student choice
10. PHON	sound	student choice
11. POST	after	student choice
12. PRE	before	student choice
13. PRO	forward, before, for, forth	student choice
14. RE	back, again	student choice
15. SCRIB, SCRIPT	to write	student choice
16. SED, SID, SESS	to sit	student choice
17. SPEC, SPIC, SPECT	to look	student choice
18. SUB	under	student choice
19. SUPER	above, over	student choice
20. SYN, SYM, SYL	together, with	student choice
21. TELE	far	student choice
22. TORT	to twist	student choice
23. TRI	three	student choice
24. VER	true	student choice
25. VERT, VERS	to turn	student choice

P. 141 EXERCISE 3 REVIEW

1. prospect	a looking forward
2. chronic	continuing for a long time
3. concurred	agreed
4. edicts	official decrees
5. propensity	natural inclination
6. aversion	extreme dislike
7. spectrum	broad range
8. panacea	remedy for all life
9. prologue	introductory event
10. posterity	future generations
11. circumvent	prevent
12. unprecedented	never having happened before

P. 142 EXERCISE 1

1. viaducts	**3.** obviate	**5.** trivia
2. impervious	**4.** devious	**6.** trivializing

P. 143 EXERCISE 2 REVIEW

1. C	**6.** extrovert	**11.** C	**16.** C	**21.** C
2. aversion	**7.** C	**12.** C	**17.** C	**22.** C
3. C	**8.** C	**13.** C	**18.** C	**23.** verification
4. C	**9.** C	**14.** C	**19.** C	**24.** C
5. C	**10.** synergistic	**15.** sympathetic	**20.** C	**25.** C

P. 145 EXERCISE 2

1. irrevocable	**4.** avocation	**7.** invocation	**10.** vocation
2. evoke	**5.** vociferous	**8.** convocation	
3. invoked	**6.** evocative	**9.** revoked	

P. 145 EXERCISE 3 REVIEW

1. C	**4.** C	**7.** C	**10.** C
2. C	**5.** C	**8.** C	**11.** C
3. bilateral	**6.** C	**9.** C	**12.** acrophobia

PP. 146–147 COMPREHENSIVE TEST A

1. A, AN	not, without	student choice
2. AMBI, AMPHI	around, both	student choice
3. ANN, ENN	year	student choice
4. ANTE, ANTI	before	student choice
5. ANTHROP	human	student choice
6. ANTI	against, opposite	student choice
7. AUTO	self	student choice
8. BENE	well, good	student choice
9. BI	two	student choice
10. BIO	life	student choice
11. CEDE, CEED	go, yield, give away	student choice
12. CHRON	time	student choice
13. CIRCUM	around	student choice
14. COM, CON, COL, COR	together, with	student choice
15. CRED	to believe	student choice
16. CUR	to run	student choice
17. DICT	to speak	student choice
18. DIS, DI, DIF	not, away, apart	student choice
19. EQU	equal	student choice
20. EU	good, well	student choice
21. EX, ES, E	out	student choice
22. FID	faith	student choice
23. GEN	birth, race, kind	student choice
24. GRAPH, GRAM	to write	student choice
25. HYPER	over, above	student choice
26. LOG	speech, word	student choice
27. -LOGY	study of	student choice
28. LOQU, LOC	to speak	student choice
29. MAL	bad	student choice
30. METER, METR	measure	student choice
31. MIT, MIS, MISS	to send	student choice
32. MONO	one	student choice
33. MORPH	form	student choice

34.	PAN	all	student choice
35.	PATH	feeling, suffering	student choice
36.	PED	foot	student choice
37.	PHIL	to love	student choice
38.	PHOB	fear	student choice
39.	PHON	sound	student choice
40.	POST	after	student choice
41.	PRE	before	student choice
42.	PRO	forward, before, for, forth	student choice
43.	RE	back, again	student choice
44.	SCRIB, SCRIPT	to write	student choice
45.	SED, SID, SESS	to sit	student choice
46.	SPEC, SPIC, SPECT	to look	student choice
47.	SUB	under	student choice
48.	SUPER	above, over	student choice
49.	SYN, SYM, SYL	together, with	student choice
50.	TELE	far	student choice
51.	TORT	to twist	student choice
52.	TRI	three	student choice
53.	VER	true	student choice
54.	VERT, VERS	to turn	student choice
55.	VIA	way	student choice
56.	VOC, VOKE	to call, voice	student choice

PP. 148–149 COMPREHENSIVE TEST B

1. B	8. D	15. C	22. D	29. A
2. C	9. A	16. D	23. C	30. C
3. D	10. D	17. D	24. B	31. C
4. C	11. C	18. B	25. A	32. C
5. B	12. A	19. A	26. C	33. A
6. C	13. C	20. D	27. C	34. A
7. A	14. D	21. C	28. B	35. C

PP. 150–151 COMPREHENSIVE TEST C

1. AMPHI both, BIO life. — an animal that lives both in water and on land; a plane that can land on water or on land
2. ANTE before. — to occur before something else
3. ANTHROP human, MORPH form. — thought of as having human form or characteristics
4. ANTI against, BIO life. — a substance used against living microorganisms
5. A not, SYM together, METR to measure. — not having both sides equal
6. AUTO self, GRAPH to write. — one's signature
7. BENE good, DICT to speak. — a blessing
8. BI two, ENN year. — occurring every two years
9. CHRON time, METER measure. — an instrument for measuring time, especially in navigation
10. CIRCUM around, SCRIB to write. — to confine
11. COL together, LOQU to speak. — informal
12. CON together, VERT to turn. — to cause to turn from one belief to another
13. CRED to believe. — believable
14. E out, MISS to send. — a person sent out on a specific mission
15. EQU equal. — to represent as equal
16. EU good, PHON sound. — pleasing sounds
17. E out, VOC to call. — to call forth, as memories or feelings
18. EX out, PED foot. — *lit.* foot out of an entanglement; useful in getting a desired result

19. FID faith.
20. GEN race, -LOGY study of.
21. MAL bad.
22. MONO one, GRAM to write.
23. PAN all, DEM people.
24. PHIL love, ANTHROP human.
25. PHOB fear.
26. PRO before, LOG speech.
27. PRO forward, SPECT to look.
28. RE back, TORT to twist.
29. SUB under, SID to sit.
30. SUPER above, ANN year.
31. TELE far, PATH feeling.
32. TRI three, VIA way.
33. VER true.
34. A, AN without, MORPH form.
35. CON (intensive), CEDE yield, go, give away.
36. PAN all.
37. SYM, SYN together, with.
38. HYPER over, above.
39. VOC, VOKE to call, voice.
40. PRE before, CEDE go, yield, give way.

faithfulness
the study of family descent
a disease
letters entwined into one design
widespread
helping humanity with charitable donations
an excessive or illogical fear
a speech before a play; an introductory event
a summary of a proposed venture
a reply to an insult or criticism
to settle down
retired because of age
the supposed communication of two people far apart
unimportant matters
to prove something is true
without definite form or shape
to acknowledge, to yield
remedy for all life
council or assembly
exaggeration for emphasis or effect
noisy
to come, go, or exist in time, order, rank, or position

WORD INDEX